# Ways of Learning

## Learning Theories and Learning Styles in the Classroom

Alan Pritchard

 **David Fulton** Publishers

David Fulton Publishers Ltd
The Chiswick Centre, 414 Chiswick High Road, London W4 5TF

www.fultonpublishers.co.uk

First published in Great Britain in 2005 by David Fulton Publishers.

10 9 8 7 6 5 4 3 2 1

Note: The right of Alan Pritchard to be identified as the author of this work has been asserted by him in accordance with the Copyright, Designs and Patents Act 1988.

Copyright © Alan Pritchard 2005

*British Library Cataloguing in Publication Data*
A catalogue record for this book is available from the British Library.

David Fulton Publishers is a division of Granada Learning, part of ITV plc.

ISBN 1 84312 323 1

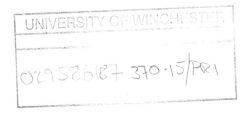
Typeset by FiSH Books
Printed and bound in Great Britain

# Ways of

Learning

THE UNIVERSITY OF
WINCHESTER

Also available:

*Learning on the Net*
*A Practical Guide to Enhancing Learning in Primary Classrooms*
Alan Pritchard
1 84312 082 8

*Help Students Improve their Study Skills*
*A Handbook for Teaching Assistants in Secondary Schools*
Jane Dupree
1 84312 263 4

*Cognitive Styles and Learning Strategies*
*Understanding Style Differences in Learning and Behaviour*
Richard Riding
1 85346 480 5

*School Learning and Cognitive Style*
*Richard Riding*
1 85346 694 8

# Contents

To Mum and Dad, who set me on the road to learning, and to Jackie, Maria and Frances, who have taught me far more than I ever could have imagined possible. Thanks.

# Preface

Learning is something that happens quite naturally and goes by quite unnoticed in many cases. We may reflect on the way that a child is able to do something which previously they could not and we may be amazed at the way that a young child has developed over even a short period of time. This is unplanned learning, though parents often spend time helping children to develop certain skills and understanding, and as such it is recognised as different to the planned learning that takes place in the more formal settings of our educational system – playgroups, nurseries and schools.

As children develop, they follow what is sometimes considered a 'normal' pattern of learning, and they become more skilled and knowledgeable almost as a matter of course. However, in order to enhance this process we have an established system whereby children are taught and where they are initiated into the accepted knowledge and skills base that is considered to be essential if they are to grow into citizens of our society who are able to function and contribute effectively, as well as lead happy and fulfilling lives.

The nature of the accepted knowledge and skills is not a topic for consideration here, but the means by which the initiation takes place, in particular the ways in which learning progresses and the most effective approaches which teachers might employ, are at the heart of this book. Learning in schools does not happen by chance, though children will learn many things that are not planned for, and an understanding of the ways in which we believe learning takes place is really an essential for those responsible for planning and implementing programmes of learning – our teachers.

Our understanding of the processes involved in learning is developing as more and more focused research is undertaken. This research takes place both in laboratories remote from schools, and in classrooms where teachers are engaging daily with an enormous range of topics, with an enormously variable population of learners. In the laboratories, the research might focus on the structure of the brain, for example, and in classrooms the research might focus on techniques of questioning or perhaps the effect of the immediate environment on the ability of children to concentrate. When all of the findings, however tentative some of them might be, are considered together, and when some of the assumptions from research are tested and re-examined in more detail, we are able to arrive at a generally accepted set of approaches to teaching which seem to be effective. This set of approaches is wide, variable and constantly shifting. That is to say, there is not a one-size-fits-all answer to the questions 'How do children learn?' and 'How should teachers teach?'

The purpose of this book is to review what is known about the ways that learning can take place and to present the views and theories of those researchers and practitioners who have been able to make detailed studies of the processes and complexities involved in learning – that is, gaining knowledge, developing understanding and acquiring skills.

We will consider some of the earliest attempts to understand learning, beginning with the behaviourist approaches made at the turn of the twentieth century. These theories have proved effective in providing approaches to teaching over many years, but in a large number of areas have been superseded by theories that take a broader stance on such things as mental activity, the importance of prior knowledge, social context and social interaction through the medium of language. An individual's preferred manner of working – learning style – is also an area of investigation which has developed to the point where it is possible to describe and observe what are sometimes quite big differences in the ways in which learners might make progress according to the ways in which they are expected to work. We will consider the more recent findings of research into the structure and functioning of the brain and look at the ways in which an understanding of the physiology, as opposed to the psychology, of the brain can lead to changes in the ways that we develop teaching strategies that we perceive as effective.

At each stage we will look at some of the practical implications of the research and beliefs that are disseminated and promoted by those working in the different fields of educational development and other related disciplines. For teachers, the most important aspects of the findings of research are related to what they can do in their planning and teaching in order to improve and enhance the learning experiences and outcomes of those in their educational charge. When teaching is based soundly on the best available understanding of the processes that lead to effective learning, it has a greatly improved chance of being effective. This book aims to provide that best available understanding. In doing so, the hope is that teachers might be able to provide even better learning opportunities for their pupils.

# Chapter 1

## Learning

Learning is something of which we all have an understanding and in which we have all participated. This participation has been in a very wide range of settings, both formal and informal, ranging from the relative confines of a school classroom, to the wide open spaces of the countryside or a quiet corner where a chance conversation led to deeper understanding of some topic or another.

Learning is not exclusive to the domain of an education system. Learning begins a very long time before school; continues for even longer after school; and happens rapidly, and in parallel with school, in a great number of different ways and settings. Learning proceeds in a number of different ways, and has been described and explained by many different interested researchers and opinion-makers over many years.

## How is learning currently defined?

Without looking for too long, and without delving too deeply into learned sources, it is possible to find a range of definitions of the process of learning. Table 1.1 contains a sample of these definitions.

Each of us will identify more or less strongly with different definitions from the list presented. In everyday terms, it is supposed that learning is the process of gaining more knowledge, or of learning how to do something – ride a bike, for example. As we will see, learning is viewed differently by those who have spent time investigating and experimenting in the field, according to the context of their work and other factors exerting influence at the time. We will look at the work of both behaviourist and cognitive psychologists and consider the very different approaches that

**Table 1.1** Definitions of learning

A change in behaviour as a result of experience or practice.

The acquisition of knowledge.

Knowledge gained through study.

To gain knowledge of, or skill in, something through study, teaching, instruction or experience.

The process of gaining knowledge.

A process by which behaviour is changed, shaped or controlled.

The individual process of constructing understanding based on experience from a wide range of sources.

each takes and the very different definitions that each might offer of a process which, for most of us, comes very naturally.

A basic understanding of processes of learning is essential for those who intend to develop activities that will have the potential to lead to effective learning taking place in classrooms, that is teachers. In more recent times, there has been a reduction in the emphasis given to learning about 'learning', from a theoretical standpoint, in initial courses for teacher education in the United Kingdom. This has been for a variety of reasons. For example, in recent years there has been a proliferation of regulations from central government which has made great demands on the training providers and substantially squeezed the time available for teaching. There has also been an emergence of alternative entry routes into teaching; some of which can be called 'work-based'. This too has led to a reduction of the time available for theoretical work. To be fair, and in the view of most of those involved in teacher education, the balance between practice and theory has been improved, but this has been at the expense of some areas of teaching which have traditionally made up the curriculum for initial training courses.

The last years of the twentieth century and the beginning of the twenty-first have seen a great deal of regulation aimed at the institutions responsible for the training of teachers. In tandem with this, there has been a big increase in the level of accountability to government, through the medium of the Teacher Training Agency (TTA) and through the inspection of teacher training by the Office for Standards in Education (Ofsted). This has been a political drive towards raising standards in schools; improving the quality of teachers; and arriving at consistency and uniformity among the trainers which had previously been missing. The outcome of these reforms seems to have been that teachers in training are not always fully introduced to more than introductory ideas of learning theory which underpin the approaches taken by effective teachers. In some cases, trainees are not always introduced to recent and current ideas relating to learning, such as those which are considered in later chapters. Though only anecdotal, it seems that some recently qualified teachers, when introduced to basic ideas from learning theory as a part of a higher degree programme of continuing professional development, have expressed surprise that this had not been covered in their initial training. Some would argue that initial training is not the place to dwell on what can be seen as uncontextualised theory, and that after some time in post, when theory can be related very directly to practice, is the best time to consider theory or, at least, to revisit it.

The current standards that trainee teachers have to meet in order to obtain Qualified Teacher Status (QTS) (TTA 2003) do not explicitly refer to learning theory, but some of the standards, if they are to be met effectively, rely on more than a passing familiarity with theory and research. For example, Standard S2.4 requires that trainees should 'understand how pupils' learning can be affected by their physical, intellectual, linguistic, social and emotional development'. A part of Standard S3.3.3 requires that trainees are able to teach using interactive teaching methods and collaborative group work and promote active and independent learning. Certainly it is possible to encourage all of the above in trainees, but to approach it without considering the underlying theory would be to leave the job only half completed and provide the trainees with little understanding of the reasons for such approaches.

## A brief historical perspective

Although the history of a philosophical interest in learning can be traced back to Ancient Greece, the modern history of the psychology of learning dates back to the late nineteenth and early twentieth centuries. William James, an American philosopher and physician, is considered to have been in at the very beginning of the serious study of mental processes. He said, in 1890, that psychology was the 'science of mental life'. It is from this approximate starting point that the study of the mind and of human behaviour, and in particular the study of learning, began to grow.

Early interest in learning, or training, was centred purely on behaviour. As we will see, the followers of this work developed the area of learning psychology referred to as 'behaviourism'. Behaviourism developed rapidly through the early years of the twentieth century and almost, but not quite, alongside this growing interest in behaviour and the modification of behaviour came the growing realisation that the unseen mental processes involved in learning, and the contribution of factors apart from environmental rewards or gratification, had an important bearing on the understanding of how we learn.

So, in very general terms, two branches of the psychology of learning developed and have made important inroads into the practice of teaching over the last decades. First there is behaviourism, and second 'constructivism', which is an aspect of a very much larger field of understanding and study, that of cognitive psychology. Both of these branches have a series of sub-branches, but it is reasonably fair to divide learning theory in this way. As we will see, behaviourism is concerned with what can be seen happening – behaviour. Constructivism rests on the idea that knowledge and, more importantly, understanding are constructed by individual learners and an understanding of the mental processes involved; the underlying structures relating to knowledge and understanding are deemed to be of prime importance.

## Other developments

An aspect of the learning process that in relative terms has only recently come to the fore is that of individual learning preferences. The ideas that lie behind the notion that we as individual learners have preferred approaches to our learning are based upon research which identifies humans as more or less receptive to different stimuli. For example, one learner might find it particularly straightforward to take in information through one particular medium and another learner would find this quite difficult. This leads to a classification of learning types which describes learners in such terms as 'visual' or 'auditory' learners, to name but two. Other researchers have developed other types of classifications which emphasise other characteristics. This whole area of individual preference or propensity for different approaches to learning has the potential to make a big impact on what happens in classrooms.

An important development in our understanding of how learning proceeds was the publication of Howard Gardner's work on what he has called 'multiple intelligences'. He describes a picture of a set of different intelligence strengths, including areas such as linguistic, mathematical, physical and more, which we all have in different proportions, giving each of us a different profile of intelligences which will affect the way in which we approach problems and the ease with which we might understand new ideas according to how they are presented.

Metacognition is another example of the development of our realisation that learning is a vast and complex subject. 'Metacognition' refers to knowledge and thought about learning itself. It is proposed that if an individual learner is able to gain insight into their own thought processes and come to better understand the ways in which they learn then they are better equipped as learners and likely to make good progress at times when they might otherwise find learning less straightforward.

The last developing area of knowledge about learning, which we will mention here and develop in Chapter 6, is that of what is widely known as 'brain-based learning'. This refers to a body of knowledge taken from a range of disciplines, including neuroscience and educational research, which gives insight into approaches that appear to favour learning and that rely on what is known about brain structure and function. Brain-based learning is a fusion of many ideas and approaches, many of which are taken very seriously by teachers in a range of different settings.

# Chapter 2

## Behaviourism and the Beginnings of Theory

The ideas of behaviourism have their roots in the late nineteenth and early twentieth centuries. John B. Watson, an American working in the realm of the new psychology, is widely accepted as one of the earliest proponents of behaviourism. He is believed to have first used the term 'behaviourism' (though he probably used an American spelling). Watson came to the view that psychology could only ever become a true science if it became a process of detailed objective observation and scientific measurement. This notion of observation and measurement became central to the work of behaviourists. Any consideration of mental process, which is by definition unobservable, fell outside of their self-imposed range of interest. So behaviourist approaches to, and explanations of, learning developed out of the study of what can actually be seen. As we will see, this approach to developing a psychological theory of learning ignores much of the hidden mental process which later workers in the field have come to explain and to hold as crucially important to our understanding of the complex activity that makes up different types of learning.

Behaviourism is based around the central notion of a reaction being made to a particular stimulus. This apparently simple relationship has been used to describe even the most complex learning situations. At its simplest, we can observe behaviour, which we can refer to as 'learnt behaviour', in a wide range of diverse situations. For example, a performing seal will respond to a particular stimulus – the sound of a hooter or the presentation of a fish – by raising itself up and slapping its flippers together as if clapping. A pet dog will respond to the stimulus of the spoken word, 'Beg', by doing just that, much to the delight of onlookers.

This stimulus-response relationship can also be seen in humans. In situations where an immediate response is required, practice situations are repeated endlessly so that the soldier, firefighter or airline pilot will make the correct, possibly life-saving response in a given situation. The importance of responsive practice has been underlined in more recent years and explained in terms of the reinforcement of particular neural pathways in the brain, which has the effect of faster and smoother implementation of certain actions and responses. The adage 'practice makes perfect' seems to hold good for behaviourists and neuropsychologists alike. In schools we notice an obvious response to the signal marking the end of a lesson. No matter how many times the teacher might remind a class that the bell is a signal for the teacher, the class can hardly restrain themselves from collecting their pens and pencils together ready to leave. Also in the classroom, a child might respond to the stimulus of the question, 'What are seven eights?' with the automatic response, '56'. This immediate 'correct' response will be made if the connection between the stimulus and response has been built correctly in the first instance, and subsequently reinforced over time; the associated neural pathways have been practised and strengthened. It should be noted here that making a 'correct' response does not necessarily imply understanding. In the same way as a parrot might react to the question, 'How are you?' with the response, 'I'm fine', so a child correctly responding with '56' need not necessarily understand the significance of the reply. Behaviourism is based upon the simple notion of a relationship between a stimulus and a response, which is why behaviourist theories are often referred to as 'stimulus-response' (SR) theories.

## Behaviourism: a definition

Behaviourism is a theory of learning focusing on observable behaviours and discounting any mental activity. Learning is defined simply as the acquisition of new behaviour.

Behaviourists call this method of learning 'conditioning'. Two different types of conditioning are described and demonstrated as viable explanations of the way in which animals and humans alike can be 'taught' to do certain things. First there is classical conditioning.

# Classical conditioning

This involves the reinforcement of a natural reflex or some other behaviour which occurs as a response to a particular stimulus. A well-known example of this type of conditioning, the first of its kind, is the work of Ivan Pavlov, a Russian physiologist at the start of the twentieth century, who conditioned dogs to salivate at the sound of a bell. He noticed that dogs salivated when they ate, or even saw, food. In his initial experiments he sounded a bell at the time when food was presented to the dogs. The sound of the bell became, for the dogs, an indication that food was about to be presented and eventually the dogs would salivate at the sound of the bell irrespective of the presence of food. The dogs had been conditioned to respond to the sound of the bell by producing saliva. Their behaviour had been successfully modified.

We talk about conditioning and conditioned responses in a general way. Feelings of fear at the sound of the dentist's drill or at the sight of a syringe in preparation for an injection are examples of conditioned responses.

Pavlov identified four stages in the process of his classical conditioning and what follows from the initial connection between stimulus and response: acquisition, extinction, generalisation and discrimination.

## Acquisition

The *acquisition* phase is the initial learning of the conditioned response – for example, the dog salivating at the sound of the bell.

## Extinction

Once learnt, a conditioned response will not remain indefinitely. *Extinction* is used to describe the disappearance of the conditioned response brought about by repeatedly presenting the bell, for example, without then presenting food.

## Generalisation

After a conditioned response to one stimulus has been learnt, it may also respond to similar stimuli without further training. If a child is bitten by a dog, the child may fear not only that particular dog, but all dogs.

## Discrimination

*Discrimination* is the opposite of generalisation. An individual learns to produce a conditioned response to one stimulus but not to another similar stimulus. For example, a child may show a fear response to freely roaming dogs, but may show no fear when a dog is on a lead; or distrust Alsatians but not Jack Russell terriers.

## Operant conditioning

The second type of conditioning is 'operant conditioning'. Operant conditioning is the most important type of behaviourist learning. It is more flexible in its nature than classical conditioning and therefore seen as potentially more powerful. It involves reinforcing a behaviour by rewarding it. It can also work in a negative way, when an undesirable behaviour can be discouraged, by following it with punishment of some form. In some cases, simply not offering an expected reward for a particular behaviour is a sufficient punishment. For example, if a mother gives her child a chocolate bar every day that he tidies his bedroom, before long the child may spend some time each day tidying. In this example, the tidying behaviour increases because it is rewarded. This rewarding is known as 'reinforcement'. It is likely that the tidying behaviour would decrease or stop completely if the rewards were suspended.

Skinner, a psychologist working in America in the 1930s, is the most famous psychologist in the field of operant conditioning and probably the most famous behaviourist. Skinner studied the behaviour of rats and pigeons, and made generalisations of his discoveries to humans. He used a device now called a Skinner box. The Skinner box was a simple, empty box in which an animal could earn food by making simple responses, such as pressing a lever. A normal, almost random action by the animal, such as pressing a lever in the box, would result in a reward, such as a pellet of food. As the rewards continued for the repetition of the action, the animal 'learnt' that in order to be fed it must press the lever.

Skinner maintained that rewards and punishments control the majority of human behaviours, and that the principles of operant conditioning can explain all human learning. The key aspects of operant conditioning are as follows.

## Reinforcement

This refers to anything that has the effect of strengthening a particular behaviour and makes it likely that the behaviour will happen again. There are two types of reinforcement: positive and negative.

## Positive reinforcement

Positive reinforcement is a powerful method for controlling the behaviour of both animals and people. For people, positive reinforcers include basic items such as food, drink, approval or even something as apparently simple as attention. In the context of classrooms, praise, house points or the freedom to choose an activity are all used in different contexts as rewards for desirable behaviour.

## Negative reinforcement

As its name suggests, this is a method of decreasing the likelihood of a behaviour by pairing it with an unpleasant 'follow-up'. There is controversy about whether punishment is an effective way of reducing or eliminating unwanted behaviours. Laboratory experiments have shown that punishment can be an effective method for reducing particular behaviour, but there are clear disadvantages, especially in classroom situations. Anger, frustration or aggression may follow punishment, or there may be other negative emotional responses.

## Shaping

The notion of shaping refers to a technique of reinforcement that is used to teach animals or humans behaviours that they have never performed before. When shaping, the trainer begins by reinforcing a simple response which the learner can easily perform. Gradually more and more complex responses are required for the same reward. For example, to teach a rat to press an overhead lever, the trainer can first reward any upward head movement, then an upward movement of at least three centimetres, then six and so on, until the lever is reached. Shaping has been used to teach children with severe mental difficulties to speak by first rewarding any sounds they make and then gradually only rewarding sounds that approximate to the words being taught. Animal trainers use shaping to teach animals. In classrooms, shaping can be used to teach progressively complex skills, and more obviously to ensure the desired behaviour from children at such times as the end of the day, lining up for assembly and so on. When a teacher says something like, 'Let's see which table is ready', it would not be unusual in many classrooms to witness many if not all of the children sitting up straight with folded arms, having tidied away their belongings.

There is a place for learning in classrooms that relies on the principles of behaviourism. However, since behaviourism gives little importance to mental activity, concept formation or understanding, there are difficult problems to overcome when setting out philosophies of teaching and learning that depend wholly upon behaviourist approaches.

## Behaviourism in general learning situations

As all parents will understand, there are certain situations where, for reasons of safety, it is important that young children do not do certain things – stepping off the kerb, poking electrical sockets, reaching towards a pan of cooking vegetables and so on. In a potentially dangerous situation, a parent is likely to respond swiftly and decisively. Often the action taken by a parent will involve a shouted 'No!' or the rapid removal of the child from the situation. The child will come to associate the poking of an electrical socket with an undesirable reaction from the parent and in this way learn to avoid the reaction by not poking sockets – at least, that is the expectation. The reason for no longer carrying out socket-poking is not dependent upon an understanding of the dangers of electrocution. The cessation of the poking behaviour can be described in terms of negative reinforcement. Had the parental response to the action been a smile and a hug, it is possible that the action would be positively reinforced and the chances of repetition increased significantly. This is not to recommend shouting, smacking or any such extreme action, but it can be seen that for reasons of expediency and future safety, a behaviourist response serves well. Indeed, attempting to explain the nature of possible outcomes from particular actions becomes very difficult when such concepts as severe injury or death come into the equation. The eradication of the behaviour is the most important consideration; the concepts involved become far less important. Some might argue that knowing to do or not to do something is, initially at least, far more important than understanding; the understanding can follow along behind at a more appropriate time in the intellectual development of the child.

## Behaviourism in 'school learning'

To apply models of behaviourism in the classroom, it is necessary to have clear ideas of the behaviours (operants) to be encouraged and reinforced. These behaviours could be either related to general behaviour (in the 'good/bad behaviour' sense of the word), or more educational content-related – spellings, tables and so on. The nature of the reinforcement also needs to be established. Rewards can be widely variable in nature – ticks and written comments in books; stars, stamps and stickers; more formal points or commendations possibly leading to higher level rewards such as certificates; verbal and public praise; extra privileges; sweets.

### Considerations for the use of rewards

- The rewards need to have value to the children.
- If rewards come unexpectedly, intrinsic motivation will remain high.
- If extrinsic rewards are used, it is important that everyone receives one for their best efforts. Rewarding only the 'best' is not a satisfactory approach, as it is vital to maintain high self-esteem, especially with the less able and lower attaining children.
- Rewards can be used to invigorate or add fun to an activity.

### Problems in using extrinsic rewards

- Rewards can belittle or demean a learning experience.
- Rewards can engender feelings of unfairness or competition.
- Rewards can detract from the real issue involved in completing tasks.

- Rewards do not always lead to higher quality work.
- Rewards may isolate children who feel they have little chance of getting a reward.

Critics of the application of behaviourist approaches make two main points. First that rewarding children for all learning is likely to cause the child to lose interest in learning for its own sake. Studies have suggested that using rewards with children who are already well motivated may lead to a loss of interest in the subject. Second, using a reward system or giving one child increased attention may have a detrimental effect on the others in the class. Using a behaviourist approach in the classroom seems to be most effective when applied in cases where a particular child has a history of academic failure; where there is very low motivation and high anxiety; and in cases where no other approach has worked.

Teachers find, and research (for example, Elliot & Busse 1991) also indicates, that rewarding aids the reinforcement of appropriate classroom behaviours, such as paying attention and treating others well; decreases misbehaviour; and makes for a more orderly atmosphere which is conducive to learning. The creation and maintaining of a supportive atmosphere conducive to work and attainment is a prerequisite for effective teaching. The standards that apply to the award of QTS in the United Kingdom require that trainee teachers demonstrate that they are able to: 'promote positive values' (Standard S1.3) and 'establish a purposeful working environment' (Standard S3.3.1) (TTA 2003). Subtle behaviourist approaches can be a useful tool for teachers in this area of their role.

Since it seems to be the case that the more often a stimulus and response occur in association with each other, the stronger the habit will become, a concentration on repetition seems to be a reasonable approach to take in certain learning situations. This repetition is seen in the drill and practice tutorials often associated with the learning of basic skills. An example of behaviourism taking on a major role in a drill and practice situation came with the onset of the introduction of computers into classrooms. With 'drill and practice' software, children are routinely presented with several answers to a question and with each correct response they receive some type of positive reinforcement (a smiley face, more fuel or more bullets to fire). With each incorrect response, children are, at best, given the opportunity to review the material before attempting to answer the question once again or, at worst, given the equivalent of a punishment in the form of a non smiley face, the loss of points or some such undesirable outcome. These types of programs allow children of varying abilities to work on exercises in their own time and at their own pace. In this way, it is said, all can achieve a similar level of competence and teacher time can be spent on teaching more complex knowledge and skills or focusing on those with particular needs. It has to be said that many children do find this style of presentation of work motivating and for some the learning benefits, in terms of test scores, for example, are clear. There are, as we have seen, questions concerning understanding and conceptual development. The use of individualised, behaviouristic learning, mediated by computers, in the form of an Integrated Learning System (ILS), has become a feature of some developments in ICT-supported learning environments, as we will see later.

Skinner urged educators to focus on reinforcement and on success rather than on punishing failure. In many cases, those who benefit most from approaches based on behaviourist notions are those who are less well motivated, have high anxiety or a history of failure. It must be remembered that these techniques do not work well for everyone. Bright children can find programmed instruction or simplistic drill and practice situations unsatisfying and even boring. Some children crave understanding and find answers without understanding difficult and frustrating.

The idea of learning without understanding, mentioned briefly above, has at times been transported directly into the classroom. Some readers may well remember being told how to divide one vulgar fraction by another by turning one of the fractions 'upside down' and then multiplying them together. This approach to teaching and being able to achieve right answers is fine for some, but for others it seems like some sort of voodoo spell and can lead to a high level of frustration. Some need to know why certain apparent 'tricks' work; without understanding the logic, they cannot operate. This was summed up by the maths educator Arnold Howell when he quoted a not uncommon rhyme used to help remember the trick for dividing one fraction by another: 'Ours is not to reason why, just invert and multiply.'

Behaviourism, then, is based on the idea that learning is a change in behaviour and that changes in behaviour occur as a response to a stimulus of one kind or another. The response leads to a consequence, and when the consequence is pleasant and positive then the behaviour change is reinforced. With consistent reinforcement, the behaviour pattern becomes conditioned.

An example might involve teaching a child to say 'please' and 'thank you' appropriately. If the child is hungry and sitting at the table, the parent might have the child say, 'please' when offered food and 'thank you' when it is taken. If 'please' is not given, the food is withheld. When 'please' is finally given up by the child, the food is served. Over the course of many meals, the child's response to the stimulus becomes conditioned and a lifelong pattern of saying 'please' and 'thank you' at suitable times becomes established.

Many modern learning theorists and educationalists discount a great deal of behaviourist theory. However, there are situations where a behaviourist approach is likely to work well. Programmed learning was developed out of the theories of Skinner and others, and became a fashionable and partly successful approach to teaching in the middle part of the last century. Skinner (1958) described the purpose of programmed learning as being to 'manage human learning under controlled conditions'. In practice, this would mean that a textbook or, as the technology allowed, a computer presents material to be learnt in a series of small steps, each step known as a 'frame'. Each frame would contain an item of information and a statement with a blank space to be completed by the learner. The correct answer would next be uncovered by moving a paper down the page, or by some such process, before the learner would move on to the next frame. Each frame would introduce a new idea or review what had gone before. The learner's response, compared with the uncovered answer, serves to reinforce correct responses, making it likely that they will be repeated and internalised. The process of shaping is employed, in that the programme of learning starts from the learner's initial knowledge then moves forwards in small increments. The learner is usually, as a result of the progression being made in very small steps, able to give accurate and correct responses which are continually positively reinforced, which will have the effect of keeping motivation high. Skinner emphasised the reinforcement given by the 'machine' for every correct response, and the importance of immediate feedback.

Behaviourism is clearly at the heart of, and the key to the success of, programmed learning. In more recent times, ILSs have made use of the behaviourist tradition and the processing power of modern computers to provide individualised routes through learning materials. An ILS is a computer-based system used for teaching. Lessons are organised by level of difficulty and worked through progressively by an individual learner. An ILS also includes a number of management tools for assessment, record keeping, report writing, and for providing other user information files which help to identify learning needs, monitor progress and maintain records.

By repeatedly presenting information in small amounts and by reinforcing correct responses, the ILS is operating in a way that can be traced back directly to Skinner's ideas. Becker (1993) identifies the behaviourist 'programmed learning theories of Skinner and others as those which underpin the model of learning used by Integrated Learning Systems. These theories assume the child's learning is solitary and individualistic.' Purcell (undated) points out that 'behaviourist ideas of learning certainly match the style of teaching and learning associated with the use of Integrated Learning Systems'.

The behaviourist approach which seems to be at the heart of ILSs has been a cause of concern for many; the apparent lack of understanding that is engendered by the process is also cause for concern. However, certain elements of the results in standardised tests in both literacy and numeracy have shown marked increases in many cases where ILSs have been evaluated (Underwood & Brown 1997; Underwood *et al.* 1994).

In the early days of computer use in schools, there were many examples of educational software designed wholly around behaviourist principles, as we saw earlier. Challenges would be set in spelling or in arithmetic, and a correct answer would activate a jingle and a flashing picture to indicate success. An incorrect answer would result at best in nothing, but at worst in a condemnation in the form of a screen picture of maybe a dunce's cap accompanied by an appropriate sound effect. The simplicity of many of the programs led to an approach of trial and error, or even random selection by some users, and the use of this type of program was condemned by some. For example, Daniel Chandler (1984) considered that 'The microcomputer is a tool of awesome potency which is making it possible for educational practice to take a giant step backwards.' Others have seen the benefits to particular individuals and groups of children. This is perhaps an indication that the adoption of a blanket, one-size-fits-all approach is not appropriate when we are considering the learning experiences we provide for children.

## Behaviourism in practice

In addition to using behaviourist methods in certain teaching situations, the methods can also be effective in establishing classroom behaviours. In a classroom environment, the teacher identifies the behaviours that are desirable and the behaviours that would be best discouraged. It is a somewhat natural impulse to develop punishments for those behaviours that need to be discouraged, yet research has indicated that positive reinforcements have a stronger and longer-lasting effect. Therefore, instead of devising a punishment for undesired behaviour, a reward of some kind for the preferred behaviour should be devised. When the correct actions are taken – sitting quietly, not shouting out, forming an orderly line by the door – the child is rewarded. When the incorrect action shows up, the reward is withheld. The most important element in establishing rewards is that they must be relevant to the child and be equally available to everyone in the classroom. Another consideration is that the reward can be incredibly simple. For many young children, the approval of the teacher or some public display of simple praise is reward enough. In some classrooms, more regulated systems of reward work well. We have already considered the use of a system of points leading to stars on a chart, with the possibility of an end-of-term treat or the awarding of a smiley-faced sticker serving well. Teachers often devise their own schemes for reward and some include the option to remove the reward, by deducting a point or removing the privilege in some way. The importance of a positive stance towards behaviour management is the crucial element of behaviourist 'control' and this seems to be emphasised by effective teachers. The influential McBer Report (DfEE 2000) tells us that an effective teacher 'uses rewards to influence behaviour and performance positively'.

Self-paced learning modules can be designed to take advantage of behaviourist principles. A learning experience that gives frequent feedback while the child 'learns' the material in small, bite-sized pieces is much more likely to be successful than a learning experience that simply consists of extensive reading with an end-of-term test as the only form of assessment. To further increase the likelihood of success, content can be arranged in such a manner as to 'steer' the child towards correct responses. Early success is likely to increase a child's self-esteem and add to the child's motivation to carry on. While some may find this method to be overly helpful or think of it as too much hand-holding, the end result is that the child has accomplished the goal and been able to meet specific learning objectives as planned. It is certainly the case that if behaviourist approaches were to be totally disregarded in planning for learning, a certain measure of what has been shown to be effective would be lost. However, as we will consider in later chapters, there are other theoretical perspectives that, in all probability, have more importance to the majority of learning situations, which teachers will be keen to establish. Behaviourism has a place in planning that teachers undertake, but it should most certainly not be relied upon alone as a perspective from which to plan all teaching and learning.

## A history of the names associated with behaviourism

### Pavlov

Pavlov developed the theory known now as 'classical conditioning' through the study of dogs. From his perspective, learning begins with a stimulus-response connection. In this theory, a certain stimulus leads to a particular response.

### Thorndike

Thorndike introduced a theory of learning now called 'connectionism'. Thorndike emphasised the role of experience in the strengthening and weakening of stimulus-response connections: 'Responses to a situation that are followed by satisfaction are strengthened; responses that are followed by discomfort weakened.' Thorndike proposed that practice also influences stimulus-response connections. His idea that rewards promote learning continues to be a key element of behaviourist theory.

## Watson

Watson introduced the term 'behaviourism' and was an important advocate of the approach in the early part of the twentieth century. Watson called for the use of scientific objectivity and experiment in the psychology of learning. He devised the law of frequency that stressed the importance of repetition: 'The more frequent a stimulus and response occur in association with each other, the stronger that habit will become.' He also devised the law of recency: 'The response that has most recently occurred after a particular stimulus is the response most likely to be associated with that stimulus.'

## Guthrie

Edwin Guthrie put forward a theory of what he called 'contiguity': 'A stimulus that is followed by a particular response will, upon its recurrence, tend to be followed by the same response again. This stimulus-response connection gains in its full strength on one trial.' Guthrie conducted very little practical research and as a result doubt has been cast upon his theories.

## Skinner

Skinner is probably the best known psychologist in the behaviourist tradition. He identified the theory of operant conditioning. Skinner spoke only about the strengthening of responses, not the strengthening of habits or actions. Skinner used the term 'reinforcer' instead of 'reward'. He was keen to stress the importance of a positive approach to learning involving rewards, but also understood the value of punishment. His most fundamental principle is his law of conditioning: 'A response followed by a reinforcing stimulus is strengthened and therefore more likely to occur again.' A second principle was his law of extinction: 'A response that is not followed by a reinforcing stimulus is weakened and therefore less likely to occur again.' Skinner's work was meticulous and methodical, based upon scrupulous scientific observation and measurement. He developed strict schedules of reinforcement in his attempt to codify learning and to establish a pattern of best practice. In his later work, he began to recognise the influence of mental process which had previously been acknowledged by behaviourists.

## Summary

Behaviourists see learning as a relatively permanent, observable change in behaviour as a result of experience. This change is effected through a process of reward and reinforcement but has little regard, initially, for mental process or understanding.

 **In the classroom**

- Standard routines and expectations for behaviour can be made clear and reinforced in a behaviouristic way.

- The use of rewards in the form of team points, or such like, can be a great incentive to work hard and to behave well.

- Punishments, such as loss of privileges, or the withholding of rewards can be effective as well, although it is widely recognised that a positive approach is preferable to an approach to behaviour management predicated solely on punishments.

- Some 'rote' learning may be a useful way of helping some children to cope better with some of the aspects of their work which they find difficult. Where possible, initial rote learning should be followed by attempts to encourage understanding.

It is interesting, in consideration of the basic tenets of behaviourist learning theory, to look briefly at a quotation from Lao-Tzu, an ancient Chinese philosopher of the sixth century: 'Rewards and punishments are the lowest form of education.'

This leads conveniently into the next chapter which deals with cognitive learning theory, where the place of reward and punishment is far less prominent.

# Chapter 3

## Cognitive, Constructivist Learning

## Constructivist theories

The area of constructivism, in the field of learning, comes under the broad heading of cognitive science. Cognitive science is an expansive area. It has its roots in the first half of the twentieth century at a time when academics from the disciplines of psychology, artificial intelligence, philosophy, linguistics, neuroscience and anthropology realised that they were all trying to solve problems concerning the mind and the brain.

## Cognitive science: a definition

Cognitive scientists study (among other things) how people learn, remember and interact, often with a strong emphasis on mental processes and often with an emphasis on modern technologies. Cognitive science investigates 'intelligence and intelligent systems, with particular reference to intelligent behaviour' (Posner 1984).

## Cognitive psychology: a definition

Cognitive psychology is the scientific study of mental processes such as learning, perceiving, remembering, using language, reasoning and solving problems.

## Constructivism: a definition

Constructivists view learning as the result of mental construction. That is, learning takes place when new information is built into and added onto an individual's current structure of knowledge, understanding and skills. We learn best when we actively construct our own understanding.

The reference in the preceding paragraph to knowledge, understanding and skills refers to what is commonly considered to be a description of the types of learning that we become involved with. These three areas for learning are joined by a fourth and are:

● knowledge

● concepts

● skills

● attitudes

(DES 1985)

It is within these four areas that all learning, in particular school learning, can be placed. We learn factual information; we learn to understand new ideas; we learn skills, both mental and physical; and we learn about, and develop, new attitudes to our environment.

## Piaget

Jean Piaget, who is considered to be one of the most influential early proponents of a constructivist approach to understanding learning, is one of the best known psychologists in the field of child development and learning. Many teachers are introduced to what is known as his 'developmental stage' theory, which sets out age-related developmental stages. The stages begin with the sensori-motor stage and end with the stage of formal operations. The developmental stage theory is a useful guide to intellectual growth, but modern thought has gone beyond Piaget's view. Table 3.1 sets out Piaget's stages.

During the sensori-motor period, Piaget said that a child's cognitive system is more or less limited to motor reflexes which are present at birth, such as sucking. The child builds on these reflexes to develop more sophisticated behaviour. Children learn to generalise specific actions and activities to a wider range of situations and make use of them in increasingly complex patterns of behaviour.

At Piaget's pre-operational stage, children acquire the ability to represent ideas and to engage in mental imagery. In particular they do this through

**Table 3.1** Piaget's stages of development

| Period | Age | Characteristics of the stage |
|---|---|---|
| Sensori-motor | 0–2 years | Simple reflexive behaviour gives way to ability to form schemas and to create patterns and chains of behaviour. Over time children come to realise that objects exist even if they cannot be seen. |
| Pre-operational | 2–7 years | Children are essentially egocentric and unable to consider events from another's point of view. The use of symbolic thought begins and the imagination also begins to develop. |
| Concrete operational | 7–11 years | Children begin to use logical thought about physical operations; they are able to conserve – that is, they realise that two equal physical quantities remain equal even if the appearance of one changes. |
| Formal operations | 11+ years | Children are able to think hypothetically and abstractly, although this is limited by lack of depth and breadth in knowledge. |

the medium of language. They have an egocentric view; that is, they view the world almost exclusively from their own point of view and find it difficult to consider situations from another's perspective.

In the concrete operational stage, children become more able to take another's point of view and they begin to be able to take into account multiple perspectives. Although they can understand concrete problems, Piaget would argue that they cannot deal effectively with more abstract problems.

At the stage of formal operations, children are capable of thinking logically and in the abstract. Piaget considered this stage to be the ultimate stage of intellectual development, and said that although children were still in a position of having relatively little knowledge, their thought processes were as well developed as they were ever likely to be.

Whether Piaget was correct or not, it is safe to say that his theory of cognitive development has had a great influence on all work in the field of developmental psychology. Piaget's view of a child's intellectual development has influenced teaching practices too. It gives teachers approximate guidance concerning the level of complexity that might be expected in a child's thought processes at approximate stages in their development. The exactness of the stage of development in relation to a child's age has been criticised; that is to say, a child may well pass through the stages but it is not clear that they will pass through them at specific ages. However, as a developmental trail, it is useful.

Another aspect of Piaget's work is concerned with the growth of knowledge and understanding, and the ways in which new information is dealt with by young learners. Piaget's descriptions of assimilation and accommodation, which we will consider next, are not restricted to young learners, and give a good representation of the process of learning for learners of all ages.

For Piaget, learning is a process of adjustment to environmental influences. He describes two basic processes which form this process of adjustment. They are *assimilation* and *accommodation*. Piaget's view is influenced by his background in biology and he sees organisms, including human beings, as constantly seeking to maintain a stability in their existence. A physical example of this would be the maintenance of a constant body temperature. If external conditions change – get hotter, for example – a sophisticated organism will make physical changes in order to maintain stability. The body's temperature regulation systems come into operation and a constant temperature is held. Piaget's model for learning is similar. External experiences can have an impact on what is already 'known'. It could be that a new experience can add to and reinforce 'knowledge' that is held or it could contradict existing knowledge. For example, a young child might know that a small creature covered in fur, with four legs and having a tail, is a dog. The more examples of dogs that the child comes across, the more secure this idea becomes. However, a cat is also small, furry and has a tail. New environmental experience – being introduced to a cat – contradicts the currently held knowledge and understanding concerning the definition of a dog. The new information is added to the existing information, and gradually a deeper and broader understanding of creatures with fur and tails is developed.

*Assimilation* is the process whereby new knowledge is incorporated into existing mental structures. The knowledge bank is increased to include new information.

*Accommodation* is the process whereby mental structures have to be altered in order to cope with the new experience which has contradicted the existing model.

*Equilibration* is the process of arriving at a stable state where there is no longer a conflict between new and existing knowledge.

A young child is introduced to a large white object in a kitchen and it is explained, simply, that it is hot and should not be touched. The word 'cooker' is used and remembered by the child. The child has an evolving mental structure which includes the images and ideas of a large white object, in a kitchen, the word 'cooker' and the idea that it should not be touched. Very soon after this experience, the child may well walk towards the next large white object in the kitchen, actually a fridge, and call out the word 'cooker'. When corrected by the more knowledgeable adult, a problem arises. The mental model for large white objects in kitchens is incomplete and new experience is creating a contradiction for the child. New information in the form of a simple explanation from a parent will add the new information to the existing model and learning will have taken place. The unstable has been made stable and the child can move on to a future encounter with a dishwasher or a tumble drier.

Piaget's early work formed the basis of the constructivist movement. In constructivist learning theory, the key idea is that '. . . students actively construct their own knowledge: the mind of the student mediates input from the outside world to determine what the student will learn. Learning is active mental work, not passive reception of teaching' (Woolfolk 1993).

In constructivist learning, individuals draw on their experience of the world around them, in many different forms, and work to make sense of what they perceive in order to build an understanding of what is around them.

Within constructivist theory there are, naturally, different interpretations of the basic ideas of the construction of knowledge and understanding. We will consider some of these interpretations, in particular the notion of mental frameworks which hold items of knowledge in a notional, complex structure, each item having numerous links to other related items, each link defined according to connections and interpretations constructed by the 'owner'. We will look at schema theory which gives a model of, and an explanation for, what underpins the complex process of building new knowledge and understanding.

## Schema theory

Human beings understand the world by constructing models of it in their minds.

(Johnson-Laird 1983)

Mental models, which have been described and examined by psychologists over many years (Piaget in the 1920s, Bartlett in the 1930s, Schank in the 1970s, Rumelhart in the 1980s, to mention but a few), and which form the basis of schema theory, are now fairly widely considered as a reasonable way of describing the way that the process of learning unfolds. Johnson-Laird tells us that mental models are the basic structure of cognition: 'It is now plausible to suppose that mental models play a central and unifying role in representing objects, states of affairs, sequences of events, the way the world is, and the social and psychological actions of daily life' (Johnson-Laird 1983) and we are told by Holland that 'mental models are the basis for all reasoning processes' (Holland *et al.* 1986).

To look more closely at the idea of a schema, we can describe it as a theoretical multidimensional store for almost innumerable items of knowledge, or as a framework with numerous nodes and even more numerous connections between nodes. At each node, there is a discrete piece of information or an idea. The piece of information can be in any one of a range of different forms – image, sound, smell, feeling and so on. Each node is connected to many others. The connections are made as a result of there being a meaningful link between the connected items. The links are personal, and identical items in the schemas of two different people could easily have very different links made for very different reasons, which could account for individuals having a 'different understanding' of a topic or idea. It is the adding of items to schemas and connecting them to other items that constitutes constructivist learning. There is no limit to the size to which a schema might grow. There is no limit to the number of connections within a schema which might be made, and there are no restrictions on how schemas might link and interconnect with other schemas. The more connections there are within and between schemas, the more construction has taken place and the more it is considered that knowledge and understanding has been gained; that is, learning has taken place.

A schema can exist to represent a physical skill or action. An example of this might be related to handwriting: the correct way to construct a letter, the way in which spaces are created between words. A schema related to throwing a stone or a ball would be activated and then used as a basis for learning how to throw a javelin. The stone-throwing schema would not be directly or fully applicable in the case where a longer, heavier object to throw was to be used, where there are significant differences in style and posture required to be successful. However, a child with a well-developed schema related to throwing a ball or similar object would be able to develop it into a successful schema to use in a variety of 'throwing' situations.

Figure 3.1 (based on Davis 1991) is an attempt to represent a schema, though it must be understood that to draw a schema is essentially impossible. This representation is limited by many factors, space being one. The notional 'egg' schema would have numerous links to other schemas, and in itself constitute a tiny subset (or sub-schema) of a more expansive structure. This particular restricted schema would form only a very tiny proportion of the whole knowledge base of an individual.

Some of the characteristics of schemas are:

- They are based on our general world knowledge and experiences.
- They are generalised knowledge about situations, objects, events, feelings and actions.
- They are incomplete and constantly evolving.
- They are personal.

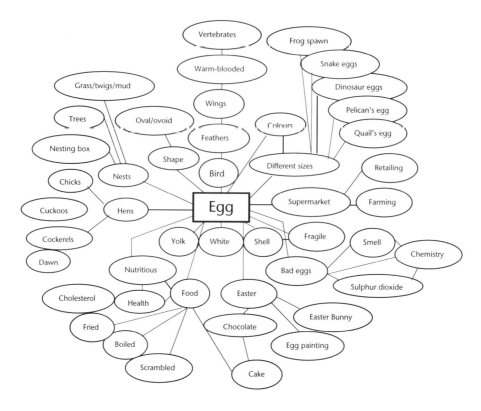

**Figure 3.1** Egg schema diagram

- They are not usually totally accurate representations of a phenomenon.
- They typically contain inaccuracies and contradictions (misconceptions).
- They provide simplified explanations of complex phenomena.
- They contain uncertainty but are used even if incorrect.
- They guide our understanding of new information by providing explanations of what is happening, what it means and what is likely to result.

Prior knowledge has a crucial part to play in constructivist learning. An existing schema represents the sum of an individual's current state of knowledge and understanding of the particular topic, event, action and so on. New learning concerned with the particular topic will involve the processes of accommodation and assimilation, and the expansion and increase in complexity of the schema in question. For this reason, it is very important that a schema that is to be the focus of these processes in the introduction of a new area of work in school is activated at the outset of a new topic, and reactivated each time the learning is to move on in subsequent lessons. In simple terms, if new learning is to take place, it is a very good idea to review what is already known about the topic in question. The starting point of what is already known and understood is very important if any new learning is to be effective. Schema activation is a process which can be encouraged in classroom situations, and teachers frequently make use of this idea in their work.

## Schema theory: a summary

Cognitive psychologists refer to units of knowledge, understanding and skill as schemas, as a way of referring to conceptual knowledge which is stored in long-term memory. It is estimated that any adult would have hundreds of thousands of schemas in memory, which would be interrelated in an extremely large and complex number of different ways. New schemas are regularly created and existing schemas are constantly updated. This creating and updating takes place every time that we read, listen to, observe, try out or sense in any other way anything new. New schemas are created every time that one fact is linked to another by a logical or semantic connection. Each schema is a sub-schema of another larger and related schema, and each schema has set of sub-schemas of its own.

Mayer (1983) gives four elements that describe a schema:

- *General:* a schema may be used in a wide variety of situations as a framework for understanding incoming information.
- *Knowledge:* a schema exists in memory as something that a person knows.
- *Structure:* a schema is organised around some theme.
- *Comprehension:* a schema contains slots which are filled in by specific information.

## Social constructivism

The origins of the constructivist view of learning have their roots in the work of Piaget. Piaget's view of the growing child was as what he called a 'lone scientist'. This description gives an image of a child alone, exploring the immediate environment, and drawing conclusions about the nature and structure of the world. Social constructivism adds an important dimension to the constructivist domain. In social constructivist theory, emphasis is placed upon interaction between the learner and others. The others can come in many forms – it is the dimension of social interaction that is crucial to the social constructivists. The main proponents of this branch of constructivism are Vygotsky, a Russian whose work was carried out at the start of the twentieth century but not widely available in the West until many years later; and Bruner, an American publishing his work in the second half of the twentieth century.

Social constructivism gives a high priority to language in the process of intellectual development. Dialogue becomes the vehicle by which ideas are considered, shared and developed. The dialogue is often with a more knowledgeable other, but this need not always be the case. Dialogue with peers can be of equal value. Prior knowledge, naturally, has a part to play. It is an individual's prior and current knowledge that forms the basis of any contribution to a dialogue. It is with reference to existing knowledge and understanding (schemas) that new ideas and understanding can be constructed in the course of dialogue. When we consider the more knowledgeable other, it is easy to assume that this person will be a teacher or a parent, but this need not be the case. More knowledgeable need not imply older nor in a position of responsibility for learning. It is very often the case that learning will take place in very different environments. Most learning does not take place in school. Any social interaction with anybody at all may well lead to learning. The building and exchange of thoughts and ideas which takes place in the course of a discussion, in any context at all, is likely for at least one of the participants, and often for both or all of them, to lead to a greater understanding of, or insight into, the topic of the conversation.

The role of the more knowledgeable other in formal learning situations is usually taken by a teacher. The teacher has the role of stimulating dialogue and maintaining its momentum. In a very real way, the teacher engages groups and individuals in dialogue and supports the development of understanding. The undertaking of this role, in a planned way, has a particular name and is known as 'scaffolding'. To fully understand the concept of scaffolding, we need to first look at an aspect of Vygotsky's work, which is the notion of a zone of proximal development (ZPD).

The zone of proximal development is a refreshingly simple description of something which many teachers and other adults understand and work with. It is an idea from Vygotsky's work which has impacted on practice over the last 20 years or so as more importance has been given to the notion of differentiation in teaching.

The zone of proximal development is a theoretical space of understanding which is just above the level of understanding of a given individual. It is the area of understanding into which a learner will move next. In the zone of proximal development, a learner is able to work effectively, but only with support. The zone is necessarily different for each individual child. The process of learning involves moving into and across the zone and looking forward to the next level of understanding, which will involve a similar journey through a newly created zone. Sewell (1990) explains it as 'a point at which a child has partly mastered a skill but can act more effectively with the assistance of a more skilled adult or peer'.

Passing through the zone of proximal development is a process which can be aided by the intervention of another. A teacher can fulfil this role and so can a range of other people or materials. In planning work for children, a teacher needs to take into account the current state of the understanding of the children in question, and plan accordingly and appropriately.

Scaffolding is the process of giving support to learners at the appropriate time and at the appropriate level of sophistication to meet the needs of the individual. Scaffolding can be presented in many ways: through discussion – a good socially constructive approach; through the provision of materials – perhaps supplying practical apparatus to help in the solution of simple problems in arithmetic; or by designing tasks which match and give help appropriate to the individual – a list of words given to help in the process of completing an exercise designed to assist understanding, or a list of reminders concerning the process of undertaking the task in question; a writing frame to support a particular style of written piece is also an example.

Working collaboratively, in pairs or small groups, is an obvious socially constructive approach to learning. The converse of this would be working in a silent classroom, where contact with others is discouraged. There are times when quiet individual working is useful and important, and teachers are able to describe times when a child should be encouraged to work quietly and alone. As a mainstay approach to teaching and learning, this would totally ignore all that we know about socially constructed learning.

## Situated learning and authentic activity

'Situated learning' refers to the fact that all learning takes place in a context. The context may or may not be familiar to the learner. If the context is unfamiliar to the learner, learning will not necessarily proceed smoothly.

Situated learning (Lave & Wenger 1991), in part, suggests that skills, knowledge and understanding which are learnt, and even mastered, in one context may not necessarily be transferred successfully to another. Another aspect of situated learning, which is more relevant here, is the notion that learning can be situated in social and cultural settings, and that if a learning activity falls beyond the cultural understanding of the learner then learning is likely, at best, to be less successful than if it had been situated in a more familiar setting. For example, giving young children the task of investigating the pros and cons of fox-hunting when their cultural setting is a deprived inner-city area where contact with the countryside, with animals, domestic or wild, and the emotions associated with the discovery of ravaged lambs or roosting hens are alien to them, is very unlikely, without exceptionally detailed and sympathetic introductions and the provision of first-hand experience, to lead to good quality learning experiences. In order to introduce the children to the ideas of making a case, and arguing for particular points of view, it would be far more reasonable to invite them to consider something within their cultural domain. The same would almost certainly be true in reverse: children brought up in a rural environment with little experience of city life might well find it difficult to understand, and learn from, notions concerning overcrowded housing estates and parents fearful of letting their children play and roam freely.

There is a link between the idea of learning being situated and the need for authentic learning tasks. Much has been written on this matter. (See, for example, McFarlane 1997.) Authentic tasks are 'tasks which pupils can relate to their own experience inside and outside of school; tasks which an experienced practitioner would undertake' (Selinger 2001). When learning is made up of authentic tasks, there is a greater probability of engagement with the task and also with the information and ideas involved with the task. Authentic tasks are likely to hold the attention and interest of the children and lead to a deeper level of engagement than with another similar but 'non-authentic' or, at least, less authentic task. This links closely with the ideas put forward by the sociocultural learning theorists. Bruner (1996), Brown *et al.* (1989) and others support the need for culturally linked and authentic learning tasks. This has the desirable effect of making the difference between learning in school and 'out-of-school learning' less well defined. Children working with new ideas in a familiar context are far more likely to engage with the ideas than if the same ideas are presented in an alien context.

## Metacognition

'Cognition' is a global term which seeks to cover all of the mental activities that serve the acquisition, storage, retrieval and use of knowledge. Cognition is the ability of the brain to think, to process and store information, and to solve problems. Cognition is a high level behaviour which is thought, in many respects, to be unique to humans. Obviously the role of cognition in the processes of learning is crucial. 'Metacognition' refers to the idea of an individual's considering, being aware of and understanding their own mental (cognitive) processes and ways of learning. It is cognition about cognition. An individual's awareness of their own thought processes will have a bearing on the way that they view their own learning and is likely, with encouragement, to lead to recognition of the ways in which they might learn most effectively.

## Metacognition: a definition

Metacognitive knowledge is the knowledge that an individual has about their own cognition, which can be used to consider and to control their cognitive processes. To work metacognitively is to consider and take active control of the processes involved in learning and thinking as they are happening.

The term 'metacognition' is most closely associated with the psychologist John Flavell (1976; 1977). He tells us that metacognition consists of metacognitive knowledge and metacognitive experiences or regulation. Metacognitive knowledge is knowledge about cognitive processes, which an individual has come to understand, and can be used to control mental processes. 'Metacognition refers to one's knowledge concerning one's cognitive processes and products or anything related to them . . . metacognition refers, among other things, to the active monitoring . . . regulation and orchestration of these processes' (Flavell 1976). Brown (1987) offers a simpler version of this when he says that 'Metacognition refers loosely to one's knowledge and control of [one's] own cognitive system.'

An example of an approach to learning spelling which is influenced by ideas from metacognition involves talking explicitly about how to learn them. In the past, at least in the experience of many of us, teachers have been known to give the instruction: 'Write down these spellings and learn them for a test next week.' This is all well and good for some children, but for others it represents an insurmountable problem – how do they learn them? We all have very different approaches to tasks of this type and some children will find a way which helps them to learn lists of spellings, but many others will not. If attention is drawn to the fact that there are ways of approaching such a task and that different individuals may find different approaches more suitable, then the door has been opened to the world of developing strategies for accomplishing particular desired outcomes. This is an example of metacognitive awareness. One child may say something like this: 'I just photograph it and then I know it.' Another may say that they can only learn the spellings by repeatedly saying them aloud to a mum or dad. Another might talk about writing and rewriting the list; yet another might well say that they have no approach and are at a loss when it comes to attempting to learn them. As teachers we cannot say which strategy will suit which child, but we can provide opportunities for a group to pool ideas and discuss them. Then children can be encouraged to experiment with different approaches. One tried and reasonably successful approach to learning spellings or foreign language vocabulary is the 'Look-Say-Cover-Write-Check' method. This involves mental activity and the necessity to hold a spelling in short-term memory as well as immediate feedback being provided. Once introduced, this method may or may not suit a particular child. It is hoped that exposure to this method, and discussion of its purpose and value, at the same time as considering possible alternatives, will allow children to decide, in a metacognitive mode, how to approach the task in question.

In a related example, sometimes children are completely lost when it comes to undertaking simple mental calculation. Individual approaches to mental calculation vary widely and some approaches seem complicated and difficult to one person but clear and simple to another. The Cockcroft Report (DES 1982) found that the ways in which adults undertook mental arithmetic tasks varied enormously and that idiosyncratic approaches were very widespread. This is wholly acceptable if arriving at the correct answer is the prime objective, but for young children, trying to find their way with mental calculation, some insight into their own approaches and processes is very important. This insight into how to think in what are, for some, difficult abstract terms is metacognitive, and very helpful in the process of learning how to undertake the task in question. Teachers can encourage approaches to develop metacognitive awareness in simple ways; for example, by asking children to describe their own approaches, and by giving value to the identification of the methods and processes followed by different individuals. Instead of being satisfied with a correct answer, a teacher can probe below the surface to discover the approach taken. This is also helpful when incorrect responses to mental calculation are given. The process of sharing and experimenting with different approaches to carrying out mental calculations in an environment that is safe and supportive can, in a socially constructive way, lead to individuals developing both a fuller understanding of their own processes of thinking and, in this case, an understanding of how to tackle particular tasks.

A consideration of which approaches best suit an individual can be of immense value at times of 'routine' learning – such times as learning spellings, practising methods in maths or other factual content which needs to be internalised – but it is possibly more valuable when revision is undertaken for exams. Knowing how to best approach learning of this type can be considered by teachers and it is important to encourage learners, at every level, to discover how they learn and what suits them individually.

Wray and Lewis (1997) single out four aspects of constructivist learning theory which they consider to be of paramount importance:

- Learning is a process of interaction between what is known and what is to be learnt.
- Learning is a social process.
- Learning is a situated process.
- Learning is a metacognitive process.

From these four aspects of constructivist theory they go on to formulate four principles for teaching:

- Learners need enough previous knowledge and understanding to enable them to learn new things; they need help making links with new and previous knowledge explicit.
- Provision should be made for social interaction and discussion in groups of varying sizes, both with and without the teacher.
- Meaningful contexts for learning are very important; it must be remembered that what is meaningful for a teacher is not necessarily meaningful for the child.
- Children's awareness of their own thought processes should be promoted.

All of what has gone before in this chapter points, more or less, to what should be a very important element of learning: that is, mental activity. Mental activity should be at the centre of our teaching methods and can be encouraged in a variety of ways. When dealing with new experiences, learning seems to proceed well if the points above are in place *and* if there is mental activity on the part of the learner.

## Mental activity

Learning is not something that others can undertake on behalf of learners. It is something that learners must do for themselves. Adults – whether teachers, trainers or parents – cannot assume that if they exert thought and effort, directed towards teaching, then learning will be the inevitable result. Learning requires effort on the part of the learner, and without some effort and some mental activity, it is very unlikely that learning will take place. In the context of constructivist theory, learning is an active, not a passive, activity. Teachers continually put into place situations in which learning is likely, but without the required effort and activity on the part of the would-be learner, the outcome is not at all certain. Howe (1999) tells us that:

> Learning always necessitates mental activities being undertaken by the individual learner . . . Learning does not always have to be deliberate, but it does always require the engagement of mental processes. The mental activities of individual students form a particularly powerful source of influence on what is actually learned.

We are also told that: 'The role of the teacher is to recognise the importance of mental activity in learning' (Chastain 1971).

## Engagement

Everything about the constructivist approach to learning, in a simple and practical way, points towards the importance of learners getting as close to the material content of what it is hoped they will learn as possible and then 'doing' something with it. By undertaking actions and activities, mental or physical, which centre on the facts, the concepts or the skills in question, learners are in a position to move forward in their learning. This 'closeness' is possible in a wide range of different ways and is sometimes referred to as 'engagement'.

For children to understand new information, they must become actively involved with it; that is, they need to engage with it. There is a five-stage model for learning, put forward by a group of Australian teachers and academics, which puts engagement at the start of the process of learning; which takes a wholly constructivist approach; and within which the importance of the individual and of activity are stressed. As we have seen, from the constructivist point of view, learning is not a passive process and so, with reference to what is known about effective learning, and with due attention paid to the notion of engagement, it is possible to map out approaches to learning that encompass the best and most effective of what is currently known about learning.

The five-stage model (Reid, Forrestal & Cook 1989) sets out a route which, if followed, is likely to provide the conditions required for learning to result:

- engagement
- exploration
- transformation
- presentation
- reflection

*Engagement* is described as 'the time during which students acquire information and engage in an experience that provides the basis for, or content of, their ensuing learning' (Reid *et al.* 1989). The next stage in the model – *exploration* – is closely related to the stage of engagement. This stage can be an open-ended process, where children follow their instincts, but possibly a more profitable approach for teachers to take with their classes is to set short tasks which develop both engagement and exploration. These tasks are designed to give the child an overview of what is contained in the information under consideration and may take many forms, including reading and writing tasks; finding things out and answering questions; more manipulative activities; matching and comparing; drawing or compiling charts or diagrams; discussing and arguing, in pairs or in groups; and many other diverse and related tasks.

*Transformation* is the stage in which information with which the child has engaged, and has explored, might be reconfigured into a form which allows for *presentation* (the next stage) but, importantly, transformed into a format which will, from the teacher's point of view, enable learning objectives to be met. From the point of view of the child, certain questions will now be able to be answered.

Transformation and the resultant presentation is not the end of the process. Time to reflect upon what has been undertaken, the process and the content, gives the opportunity for internalisation, and for a deeper level of understanding to be developed. *Reflection* can also take many forms. One common approach is to ask children to give a short presentation/explanation of what they have been doing and what they have learnt. This can take a variety of different formats, prepared for a variety of different audiences – a poster to display, a newspaper front page, a multimedia presentation, or something as simple as a 30 second explanation of what they have been doing in the lesson, possibly including what they have learnt. This idea has become a part of the plenary session which now forms an integral part of lessons, especially concerning literacy and numeracy, in British primary schools.

Bereiter and Scardamalia (1987) describe a model of the writing process which they term 'knowledge transformation'. Knowledge transformation can be seen as the reshaping or reconstruction of information in order to answer certain questions, to help meet particular learning objectives and to assist the learner in the process of coming to understand the content of their learning activity. This model is characterised by the writer alone accomplishing what is normally accomplished through the medium of social dialogue. Knowledge is considered and 'worked upon' by the individual – engagement takes place. This dialogue, which forms an important element of the thinking that underpins social constructivism, is seen as the medium through which learning takes place. A child working alone cannot take part in an actual dialogue, which has the possibility of allowing engagement with the knowledge and ideas of the topic in question, but by undertaking a process of knowledge transformation, a similar process may come into play and effective learning may be possible.

## Encouraging engagement

We have seen that without engagement with the content of an activity, effective learning is far less likely to be the result of anything that teachers ask children to do. It can be surmised that an important element of the role of the teacher is to encourage engagement, since without some measure of involvement with information and ideas, and the undertaking of activity centred on the content (Bereiter and Scardamalia's knowledge transformation, for example), there is a greatly reduced opportunity for effective learning to take place, especially the deep learning which is the aim of most teaching situations.

There are many effective ways of encouraging children to engage with their work. Taking into account the prior knowledge of the children, the level of difficulty, the social and cultural context, and the general level of interest of the subject matter will all help with the need for engagement.

Certain guidelines can apply to the planning of lessons. Lessons:

- need a clear focus and goals, with explicit learning objectives;
- need to be based upon the pupils' existing knowledge;
- need to be set in an appropriate context;
- need to include scope for social interaction and for activity;
- need to be planned in such a way that they aim to move the pupils' learning forward (across the ZPD).

The points above can all be traced back to what is known about the way that we learn, and to the work of many psychologists and educationalists in the field of learning. It would be unrealistic to suggest that, if all of the above were in place, then effective learning is certain to result, since, as all teachers know, there are a great many variables, some of which are controllable and others that are not, which can so easily influence the outcome of any particular lesson. However, taking into account what is known about learning, and about how children learn, will increase the possibility of effective learning resulting from the activity undertaken.

## Summary

### Cognitivist definition of learning

Learning is a relatively permanent change in mental associations as a result of experience. The changes in mental associations are internal and cannot easily be observed.

### Mental activity

The importance of mental activity (engagement) for effective learning is at the heart of the way that cognitive psychologists describe and understand the process of learning.

### Essential features of constructivism

Constructivist learning theory is built around a set of important features which can be summed up as follows (after Jonassen *et al.* 1999):

- The construction of knowledge and not the reproduction of knowledge is paramount.

It is the processes that the learner puts into place and uses that are important, rather than the fact of knowing something as an end product. A learner is actively engaged with, and in control of, the learning process.

- Learning can lead to multiple representations of reality.

When learning involves the use of a variety of resources (e.g. first-hand experience, secondary sources, interactive materials, independent research, dialogue), alternative viewpoints of the subject in question are formed; this in turn can be used to foster the skills of critical thinking.

- Authentic tasks in a meaningful context are encouraged.

Authentic tasks, such as problem-solving, are used to situate learning in familiar and realistic contexts.

- Reflection on prior experience is encouraged.

Learners are prompted to relate new knowledge and concepts to pre-existing knowledge and experience, which allows the 'new' to integrate with what is known already and in this way adding to a learner's framework of understanding (schema) or amending it.

- Collaborative work for learning is encouraged.

Dialogue with others allows additional and alternate perspectives to be taken into account when developing personal conclusions. Different knowledge, points of view, and understanding can be given and considered before moving on.

- Autonomy in learning is encouraged.

Learners are given, and accept, increasing amounts of responsibility for their own learning. This happens in a number of different ways: by collaborating with others, by working on self-generated problems and by the formulating of, and testing of, hypotheses, for example.

The appendix includes a summary chart of the differences and similarities between the work of Piaget and Vygotsky.

## In the classroom

- Opportunities for mental activity are essential; this leads to deeper engagement with ideas and increases the possibility of effective, lasting learning taking place.
- Social interaction – that is discussion between pairs, groups and between teacher and pupils – is essential for the effective development of understanding.
- Learning set in meaningful contexts is far more likely to engage learners than if it is set in other, random or remote contexts. Make learning meaningful by placing it in a setting with which children can identify. For example, when teaching about time, refer to the fixed points in the school day, bedtimes or the length of football matches. This may appear trivial, but it can make a big difference.
- Encourage learners to review what they know about a new topic before embarking on new teaching. Ask questions. Remind the class of work from the previous term or year.
- Encourage learners, with appropriate guidance, to find things out for themselves.
- Gauge the processes of teacher intervention carefully so as to encourage thought processes. Telling is not teaching, but measured scaffolding is.
- Encourage learners to think about and put into words the methods or approaches that they use in the course of their work – mental arithmetic, for example, or how to prepare for a test.
- Allow time for learners to reflect upon what they have learnt. Well-managed plenaries at the end of lessons are very good for this.

# Chapter 4

## Multiple Intelligences

Howard Gardner's multiple intelligence theory (Gardner 1993) proposes the idea that we all have various levels of intelligence across a range of intellectual areas. Gardner's theory comes in part out of a concern that when intelligence is measured, the most commonly used tests (standard verbal and non-verbal reasoning tests) often do not allow those tested to demonstrate what they are really good at or where their intelligence lies. Gardner gives us a set of different *intelligences* which, as individuals, we display more or less of, according to our particular intellectual make-up. There are nine of these intelligences, which are:

- *linguistic:* enjoyment of and facility with reading, poetry and all things literary and linguistic;
- *logical/mathematical:* enjoyment of and facility with maths and science, games of strategy and any logic-based pursuits;
- *musical:* enjoyment of and facility with music – listening, playing and perhaps composing;
- *spatial/visual:* enjoyment of and facility with images, drawing, construction games and tactile puzzles such as jigsaws;
- *kinaesthetic:* enjoyment of and facility with activities that involve touch and movement, dance, sport and other practical activities;
- *interpersonal:* enjoyment of and facility with other people, communication, leadership and the ability to empathise;
- *intrapersonal:* enjoyment of and facility with self-motivation, no dependence on others, awareness of one's own feelings more than those of others – often seen as shyness;

- *naturalistic*: enjoyment of and facility with the natural world, with ability in recognising patterns and classification;
- *existential*: enjoyment of and facility with asking and examining questions about life, death and ultimate realities.

Originally Gardner described only seven intelligences, though later he established an eighth and a ninth. Also under consideration as possible human intelligences are spiritual and moral, though these are considered somewhat problematic.

An individual's particular strengths in intelligences have a direct bearing upon the way in which their learning takes place. For example, someone with interpersonal strengths would be most likely to learn effectively in a social situation where relating ideas and knowledge to others can be encouraged. The opposite might be true for an individual with low interpersonal intelligence but a strength in intrapersonal intelligence.

To be aware of multiple intelligence strengths and our preferred or most effective learning approach is to be operating at a metacognitive level, as we saw in Chapter 3.

## Multiple intelligences in the classroom

If the ideas set out by Gardner are to be taken seriously, then there are ramifications for the ways in which teachers teach and for the types of activities in which children in school are expected to take part. For example, a child with particular strengths that are not in the linguistic domain might well be disadvantaged if, without exception, the work that is expected of him or her relies heavily on being able to express ideas through words. This can also be true for children with other specific multiple intelligence strengths which are not catered for in some way, in their lessons.

There are many examples of the sort of problems that might occur when the majority of responses to school work rely on the abilities of the children to function effectively in the domains associated with one or other of the intelligences. Those with strengths in interpersonal intelligence who are expected to work in a solitary fashion; those who have kinaesthetic strengths and aptitudes and are not 'allowed' to work practically or to move around; and those with intrapersonal strengths and preferences who are required to operate as a part of a group working collaboratively to solve a problem are just three examples of the ways in which an ignorance of – or gard for – individual intelligence, in Gardner's terms, can lead to ..isadvantage.

In planning for multiple intelligences, teachers consider the range of activities related to the content of the lesson and the intended learning outcomes which will give a range of opportunities to the children's different intelligence strengths. This can be approached by seeking to answer certain questions, for example:

- *Logical/mathematical:* How can I include the use of numbers, classification, critical thinking and calculations?
- *Spatial:* How can I include pictures and diagrams, colours, art or graphs?
- *Intrapersonal:* How can I include private learning time and choice?
- *Interpersonal:* How can I include group work, peer sharing and discussions?
- *Bodily/kinaesthetic:* How can I include movement, practical apparatus, drama or art and craft?
- *Musical:* How can I include music, sounds, rhyme, rhythms and dance?
- *Verbal/linguistic:* How can I include reading, writing and speaking?

(Teaching and Learning for Life 2000)

It may not be possible for each and every lesson to have appropriate answers for all of the questions above, but over a period of time the planning process would allow for a balanced and – in terms of the perceived needs of the children – an equitable and suitable, 'multiple intelligence-friendly' set of classroom activities for learning.

A part of the approach taken in learning situations planned around multiple intelligences involves allowing for a wide variety of responses to particular tasks. In many school learning situations, the standard response to the investigation of a new learning topic is to write about it in a standard, almost formulaic way. In a multiple intelligence environment, set responses are not required. Often a range of different responses are encouraged and, at the least, a choice between a number of ways of recording work or other ways of dealing with new knowledge and ideas are given. The example below, from an American school, illustrates this point:

> Three eight and nine-year-old boys recently gave an oral report about California to their classmates. The students sang and danced an original song about the state, played a short video they produced, displayed maps drawn to scale and spiritedly presented a series of facts. Are these students academically advanced or exceptionally creative? No, such multi-modal learning is commonplace in a third/fourth/fifth grade multi-aged classroom at Cascade Elementary School in Maryville, WA.
>
> (Campbell & Campbell 1993)

In the description of the classroom organisation and approach to teaching employed in the classroom in the example above, we are told of different learning centres around the room where all children, in groups of three or four, spend time each day working on the topic of the day. This is a setting where the importance of the notion of multiple intelligences has been given high priority and where what might be considered a traditional approach to classroom organisation has been set aside in favour of a new approach. The article continues to describe a year-long action research project which set out to test the approach. The results, as reported, seem good, with gains noted across a range of measures, including the demonstration of increased responsibility, self-direction and independence; a significant reduction in discipline problems; improved co-operative learning; and improvement in academic achievement, measured by comparisons in grades achieved in standardised tests.

In the context of a more traditional setting, it is still possible for teachers to take multiple intelligences into account and to allow for a variety of responses to work that is to be covered. Some teachers allow for this by giving an element of choice in the way that work is recorded, for example, a written piece, a pictorial/diagrammatic piece or an audio-recording of a news item. This approach encapsulates both the notion that learners have different multiple intelligence strengths and also, as we will see in Chapter 5, that individual learners have preferred learning styles. These two areas of theory are closely related.

One approach to dealing with addressing multiple intelligences is to proceed in the usual way with planning and teaching, but to also plan for a range of follow-up activities, each set in the domain of a different intelligence. This is exemplified by Tom Hoerr in *Multiple Intelligences: Teaching for Success* (Hoerr 1996). A lesson based on the Eric Carle book *The Very Hungry Caterpillar* is described and a set of follow-up activities are presented, each of which would appeal to children with different multiple intelligence strengths. The introductory section of the lesson, where the story is read and shared with the class, is, in itself, creative and interesting, and the options for following up are diverse and give ample opportunity for individuals to work in a manner suited to their particular multiple intelligence situation.

The introduction to the lesson was creative and fun, but in many ways no different to the ways in which many teachers might choose to introduce a story and share the experience and fun of reading a story with the class. As the story, which is generally well known (Carle 2002), relates the experiences of a caterpillar which eventually transforms into a butterfly, the teacher produced a puppet caterpillar, made from a sock, and inside hid a felt model of the butterfly. At the appropriate stage, the sock puppet was removed to expose the unfolding butterfly.

The story was discussed in detail and the sequence, in particular, given special attention. Additional pictures of real caterpillars and butterflies were introduced and discussed. The children were able to relate some of their experiences concerning the story. The teacher led a discussion about the characteristics of caterpillars and butterflies, and a list of descriptive words was generated.

The story, and the added impact of the use of puppets, held the attention and interest of the class, as we would normally expect. It is in the style of activities that were presented next that the importance of individual multiple intelligence strengths is taken into account.

## Follow-up activities

- *Interpersonal:* Working in small groups, produce posters which illustrate the metamorphosis in the story.
- *Intrapersonal:* Discuss how it might feel to change from a caterpillar to a butterfly. This could be an actual discussion or a written piece.

- *Bodily/kinaesthetic:* Act out the stages of metamorphosis.
- *Logical/mathematical:* Count how many times each fruit appears in the book. Make a chart of the fruits and examine the relationship between the numbers.
- *Musical:* Crawl like caterpillars and fly like butterflies to fast/slow music.
- *Spatial:* Children make their own sock caterpillars.

Clearly the organisation of the activities could become complex, and there is a need for the teacher to take control to ensure that the activities are well supported and that appropriate numbers of children are directed towards certain activities at certain times. The bodily/kinaesthetic, for example, might well be best suited to a time when the school hall is available for PE time, but there is always the option of allowing a group to work on this at other times. The same might apply to the musical activity. The making of sock puppets could be reserved for an art lesson, or again this could be offered as an activity to choose at an appropriate time.

More detail can be found at the New City School website (New City School 2004), where there are also examples of lessons covering the full range of intelligences.

Working in the way described above may well ring some alarm bells for teachers who might assume that individual children could be in a position whereby they are given choice, and where they always choose a particular style follow-up activity and choose to avoid others – writing, for example. This is where the careful monitoring which teachers engage in becomes increasingly important. Certainly children need to be able to express themselves in the ways in which they are most expert and most comfortable, but this should not be at the expense of work in other important areas of the curriculum.

The Theories in Practice website (TIP undated), which gives overviews of many aspects of learning theory, suggests three principles which, if the ideas of multiple intelligences are to be taken seriously, should be applied in school. They are:

1. Individuals should be encouraged to use their preferred intelligences in learning.

2. Instructional activities should appeal to different forms of intelligence.

3. Assessment of learning should measure multiple forms of intelligence.

In order to apply these principles, schools would have to radically rethink many of the established processes and principles which are currently in place. For many teachers, this would present great difficulty. In schools where the established approach to teaching and learning is in some way fixed and not open to individual interpretation by individual teachers, for individual teachers to apply aspects of practice founded on Gardner's theory would be very difficult. However, to take Gardner's work into account at a less radical level is something that many teachers can do and are doing. Small changes – or at least a measure of variety – in the ways in which children are asked to work are noticeable in many situations. Recently, a secondary school in the UK, after in-service training dealing with the notions of multiple intelligences, trialled a series of different approaches to work set by teachers. In the history department, for example, when learning about the time of the First World War, the class was given a set of options concerning the ways in which they would submit work for assessment. The options included:

● creating a three-dimensional model;
● creating a set of posters;
● filming a short drama;
● using PowerPoint to present questions and answers;
● audio-recording a series of radio documentary articles.

The option to work alone, in a pair or in a larger group was also given. The possibility of presenting the end product to the class in the form of a formal presentation – a short talk, for example, or an annotated display – was also given. In themselves these options for producing an end product are not unusual, but the element of choice, which allows individuals to follow their strengths, interests or even instincts, is, for many teachers, an innovation. Choice has, for some teachers, presented a challenge. Some teachers, at times, shy away from it. In many cases there is evidence that the level of engagement with an activity, and the quality of the work produced as a result, is very high – indeed much higher than might have been expected – when choice has been allowed. The assessment of such varied end products will clearly present challenges, but not of such magnitude that they are insurmountable.

Johnson and Kuntz (1997) carried out a study of the ways in which teachers who had attended a variety of different styles of training in the use of the multiple intelligences approach responded to the ideas to which they had been introduced, once they returned to their schools. They found that overall those surveyed believed they were applying the theory in their classrooms in ways that made a significant, positive impact upon teaching and learning. They found that:

1. Multiple intelligences were used as a basis for change in their classrooms in a variety of ways:

   *Planning:* Teachers reported that they had begun to plan for teaching in ways that use as many intelligences as possible.

   *General teaching:* All teachers reported that they began to involve more intelligences in teaching.

   *Individualised teaching:* Teachers had begun to tailor teaching according to the intelligence profiles of their individual children. One teacher commented: 'Teaching must change to meet the different learning styles and strengths of my class.'

   *Self-assessment:* Teachers considered it important to teach the class about multiple intelligence theory, and encouraged them to assess and become aware of their own intelligences profile.

   *Assessment:* Teachers' views on assessment changed. One teacher said that: 'The most significant realisation I've had is that children can be assessed in many different ways.' Children were given more choice in how their learning was measured, and assessment became an ongoing and integrated part of teaching.

2. Diversity in learning is appreciated:

   *Teacher awareness:* Having been introduced to multiple intelligences, teachers were able to develop a better appreciation of the various skills of children in their class. One teacher confirmed this by saying: 'It has just brought home the fact that we are all diverse learners, and it [the application of multiple intelligence theory in their teaching] is a way that I can address that diversity.'

*Success:* An appreciation of diversity apparently began to contribute to greater involvement and more success for more children.

3. Classroom climate is more positive:

   *Co-operative:* The climate becomes more co-operative as children come to understand and gain more respect for each others' strengths.

   *Engaged:* Many teachers find that multiple intelligences-based approaches 'encourage risk-taking' and lead to a more festive, lively and creative atmosphere conducive to interest, enjoyment and achievement.

4. Multiple intelligence theory encourages self-reflection among teachers:

   *Self-validation:* Teachers learnt to accept their own intelligences, which, in turn, boosted their self-confidence as teachers.

   *Colleague appreciation:* Acceptance of personal strengths and weaknesses led to greater appreciation of other teachers' styles.

   *Risk taking:* Teachers who understood the theory of multiple intelligences developed the courage to experiment: 'I previously thought that there were certain things I simply wasn't good at.'

If the findings of this survey are to be seen as generalisable, then there is certainly merit in adopting at least some of the approaches suggested by the theory of multiple intelligences. Awareness of one's particular intelligence strengths and weaknesses is a metacognitive understanding which can contribute to a learner's ability to operate at a metacognitive level when faced with particular learning situations or when faced with problems to solve.

## Summary

● Traditional measures of intelligence stress traditionally accepted definitions of intelligence, which are based extensively on a narrow range of skills, such as reading, writing and facility with numbers.

● There are other strengths demonstrated by many individuals who are clearly 'intelligent' but not skilled with words or numbers.

- It is possible to allow children to work to their strengths at the same time as fulfilling the requirements of a set curriculum.

We will consider aspects of Gardner's thoughts on multiple intelligences in the next chapter, since an individual's strengths and preferences for learning can be affected by particular strengths or weaknesses in any of Gardner's intelligences.

The Internet is a source of multiple intelligences testing and investigation. There are many sites where it is possible to undertake a short, questionnaire-style test which will lead to the production of an individual multiple intelligence profile. Naturally the reliability of these sites must be considered, since some clearly take into account a great deal more than others when seeking out the individual's profile. A Google search using the phrase 'Test your Multiple Intelligences' returns 13 hits, each of which has either a test, an inventory of its own or a link to one on another site. Caution is advised when using these sites.

## In the classroom

- Be aware that individuals have different strengths and are likely to perform very differently according to the nature of the style of the tasks with which they are presented.
- Give opportunities for learning in a range of different ways; sitting and listening may suit some children, but others will find this particularly difficult; conversely others will not respond well to individual work. Be flexible in teaching approaches.
- Give opportunities for learners to respond in a range of different ways; writing prose responses is not the only way to record events – indeed there are many ways other than writing in which new learning can be dealt with.
- Be prepared to reward responses to work that do not necessarily conform to the traditional expectation of 'school work'.

# Chapter 5

## Learning Styles

It is apparent to many of those who have considered learning, even if only in passing, that we learn in different ways to each other and we often choose to use what has become known as a 'preferred learning style'. The literature on the subject is vast and a full review of what has been written would take in many other related areas which deal with the same, or at least very similar and very closely related, ideas. Cognitive style, for example, is an area of psychology which investigates the preferred style of thinking and problem-solving an individual may have. The term 'learning preferences' is also widely used to refer to what we shall here refer to as 'learning style'.

The literature provides many useful definitions of learning styles and related ideas which we could consider. To look briefly at one or two will act as a useful starting point.

Learning style is defined variously as:

- a particular way in which an individual learns;
- a mode of learning – an individual's preferred or best manner(s) in which to think, process information and demonstrate learning;
- an individual's preferred means of acquiring knowledge and skills;
- habits, strategies, or regular mental behaviours concerning learning, particularly deliberate educational learning, that an individual displays.

Cognitive style is also defined in a range of different ways, as:

- a certain approach to problem-solving, based on intellectual schemes of thought;

- individual characteristics of cognitive processing which are peculiar to a particular individual;
- a person's typical approach to learning activities and problem-solving;
- strategies, or regular mental behaviours, habitually applied by an individual to problem-solving.

As we can see, there are many overlapping features contained within these definitions.

So, a learning style is a preferred way of learning and studying; for example, using pictures instead of text; working in groups as opposed to working alone; or learning in a structured rather than an unstructured manner. Learning preferences refer to an individual's preferred intellectual approach to learning, which has an important bearing on how learning proceeds for each individual, especially when considered in conjunction with what teachers expect from learners in the classroom. This idea will be explored later.

The term 'learning preferences' has been used to refer to the conditions, encompassing environmental, emotional, sociological and physical conditions, that an individual learner would choose, if they were in a position to make a choice (Dunn, Dunn & Price 1989). Choice is another slant on the notion of preferred learning styles which has a bearing on how learning progresses. This is, perhaps, more to do with the more general area of cognitive preferences, but is still important in this context.

If a particular approach to learning is encouraged by a teacher, there is a possibility that some pupils will work and learn less effectively than others in the class. For this reason, an awareness of learning styles is important for teachers. Learning style awareness should make an impact on pedagogy – the ways in which teachers choose to teach – and should help teachers to a better understanding of the needs of learners, as well as to an awareness of the need to differentiate materials, not only by level of difficulty but also by learning style.

The literature dealing with learning styles has something else to say which should be of interest to teachers. It is suggested that learners who are actively engaged in the learning process will be more likely to achieve success (Dewar 1996; Hartman 1995; Leadership Project 1995). Once learners become actively engaged in their own learning process, they develop a sense of being in control. This has been shown to improve self-esteem and motivation. A learner's awareness of learning preference and an understanding of the learning process, as well as metacognitive engagement, can lead to improved learning outcomes.

## Learning styles

What becomes very clear as we think closely about different learners who are known to us, is that they do not all learn in the same way. Each individual will adopt an approach to learning with which they are most comfortable and in doing so leave behind the approaches with which they are less comfortable. It is helpful for learners if they are aware of their own particular learning preferences in order that they can use an appropriate learning style to suit the particular learning that is being undertaken, and take opportunities to improve their potential for learning when faced with a learning activity that might steer them towards one of their 'weaker' – or at least one of their less favoured – styles.

Learning styles are not fixed traits which an individual will always display. Learners are able to adopt different styles in different contexts. For most of us, one or two styles are preferred above the others. Honey and Mumford (1986) suggest that we need to be able to adopt one of four different styles in order to complete any given learning task satisfactorily. An inability or reluctance to adopt any particular style has the potential to hamper our ability to learn effectively.

The four styles described in the Honey-Mumford Model are:

● activists
● reflectors
● theorists
● pragmatists

*Activists* prefer to learn by doing rather than, for example, by reading or listening. They thrive on novelty, and will 'give anything a try'. They like to immerse themselves in a wide range of experiences and activities and like to work in groups so that ideas can be shared and ideas tested. They like to get on with things, so they are not interested in planning. Activists are bored by repetition, and are most often open-minded and enthusiastic.

*Reflectors* stand back and observe. They like to collect as much information as possible before making any decisions; they are always keen to 'look before they leap'. They prefer to look at the big picture, including previous experiences and the perspectives of others. The strength of reflectors is their painstaking data collection and its subsequent analysis, which will take place before any conclusion is reached. Reflectors are slow to make up their minds, but when they do, their decisions are based on sound consideration of both their own knowledge and opinions, and on what they have taken in when watching and listening to the thoughts and ideas of others.

*Theorists* like to adapt and integrate all of their observations into frameworks, so that they are able to see how one observation is related to other observations. Theorists work towards adding new learning into existing frameworks by questioning and assessing the possible ways that new information might fit into their existing frameworks of understanding. They have tidy and well-organised minds. They sometimes cannot relax until they get to the bottom of the situation in question and are able to explain their observations in basic terms. Theorists are uncomfortable with anything subjective or ambiguous. Theorists are usually sound in their approach to problem-solving, taking a logical, one-step-at-a-time approach.

*Pragmatists* are keen to seek out and make use of new ideas. Pragmatists look for the practical implications of any new ideas or theories before making a judgement on their value. They will take the view that if something works, all is well and good, but if it does not work, there is little point in spending time on the analysis of its failure. A strength of pragmatists is that they are confident in their use of new ideas and will incorporate them into their thinking. Pragmatists are most at home in problem-solving situations.

These four dimensions can be used as a way of classifying learners. The four basic types of learner, as characterised by preference for active, reflective, theoretical or practical learning, are clearly different one from the other, but most learners are not extreme examples of just one preference. Most people have characteristics of all four dimensions. Honey and Mumford devised a learning style inventory, designed to help individuals to find out which predominant type of learner they might be. Completing the inventory involves answering 'yes' or 'no' to 80 statements, 20 of which are related to each of the four types. The scores are then added up, plotted along the axes of a chart, and joined up to produce a kite shape of the type shown in Figure 5.1. The pattern in this diagram shows a typical pattern for a mature learner who can adopt any of the four learning styles when appropriate.

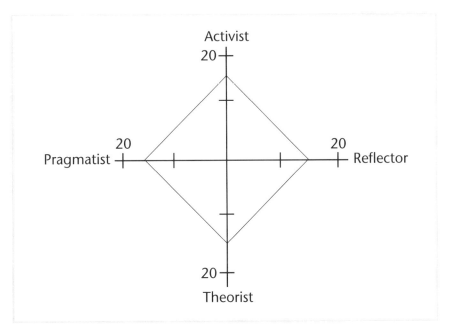

**Figure 5.1** A typical Honey and Mumford 'kite'

The next description of learning styles comes from a different, but obviously related, area of human research, namely Neuro-Linguistic Programming (NLP). Neuro-Linguistic Programming is concerned with how we communicate and how this affects our learning. Over many years, and through many research projects, including close and detailed observation of the way we communicate, three particular learning styles – visual, auditory and kinaesthetic – have been identified.

## Visual learners

Visual learners prefer to learn by seeing. They have good visual recall and prefer information to be presented visually, in the form of diagrams, graphs, maps, posters and displays, for example. They often use hand movements when describing or recalling events or objects and have a tendency to look upwards when thinking or recalling information.

## Auditory learners

Auditory learners prefer to learn by listening. They have good auditory memory and benefit from discussion, lectures, interviewing, hearing stories and audio tapes, for example. They like sequence, repetition and summary, and when recalling memories tend to tilt their head and use level eye movements.

## Kinaesthetic learners

Kinaesthetic learners prefer to learn by doing. They are good at recalling events and associate feelings or physical experiences with memory. They enjoy physical activity, field trips, manipulating objects and other practical, first-hand experience. They often find it difficult to keep still and need regular breaks in classroom activities.

While we all use all three styles of learning to some extent, some learners rely heavily on one of them. An over-reliance on one style, and an inability or unwillingness to adopt another style where it might be appropriate, can be limiting in some learning situations and can mean that learning might be hindered.

An extension of the NLP description of learning styles has been developed by Fleming (2001). Fleming tells us that when we gather information from the world around us, which includes the information that we need for learning, we make use of all of our senses. Some of us, though, employ one sense more than others. The V-A-R-K system assesses how much people rely on:

- visual
- auditory
- reading
- kinaesthetic

The Myers-Briggs Type Indicator (MBTI) system is a means of establishing an individual's personality profile and is used widely in aptitude testing for employment. Designed as a tool for investigating the many different strands of personality type, the MBTI also has something for teachers to be aware of. The MBTI describes four personality types which can be interpreted along the lines of some of the other learning style descriptions.

The Myers-Briggs Model (Briggs & Myers 1975; or Briggs Myers and Myers 1980, for example) classifies individuals according to their preferences on scales derived from the theories of psychological types developed by Carl Jung. According to the model, learners may be:

- *extroverts* – who are happy to try things out and who focus on the world of people;
- *introverts* – who are more likely to think things through and to focus on the world of ideas;
- *sensors* – who tend to be practical, detail-oriented, and who focus on facts and procedures;
- *intuitors* – who are imaginative, concept-oriented and focus on meaning;
- *thinkers* – who are sceptical, and make decisions based on logic and rules;
- *feelers* – who are appreciative and tend to make decisions based on personal and more humanistic considerations;
- *judgers* – who set and follow agendas, and seek closure and completeness even without having the full picture; or
- *perceivers* – who adapt to changing circumstances and will defer completion until more is known.

The Myers-Briggs Type Indicator type preferences can be combined to give 16 different learning style types. For example, one learner may be an E-S-T-P (extrovert, sensor, thinker, perceiver) and another may be an I-N-F-J (introvert, intuitor, feeler, judger). Across all 16 types, there is a wide range of different types of learner, all of which can be found, in different proportions, in our classrooms. One element of the Myers-Briggs work that has become more commonly used is the introvert–extrovert continuum. This is perhaps a result of the Myers-Briggs types being based on

Jung's work. Jung's main focus and subsequent work on personality types was on the introvert–extrovert dimension. The notion of an introvert or an extrovert has become widely understood outside of the world of education or spheres of psychological study. The other dimensions have not.

According to the descriptions set out by the Myers-Briggs work, the following attributes and strengths relate to each of the different types defined.

## Extrovert learners

Extrovert learners like to:

- talk to understand new information and ideas;
- work in groups;
- try something first and think about it later;
- see the results from a project;
- see examples of how other people are doing the work.

### Strengths

Extroverts learn best when they can work with a friend and learn by trying something themselves instead of watching or listening to others. When they have difficulty with understanding, they benefit by talking about their ideas with others.

## Introvert learners

Introvert learners like to:

- study alone;
- listen to others talk and think about information privately;
- think about something first and try it later;
- listen, observe, write and read;
- take time to complete assignments.

## Strengths

Introverts learn best when they can find quiet places to work and have enough time to reflect on, redraft and improve their work. Introverts often like to make connections between school work and their personal interests.

# Sensing learners

Sensing learners:

- like clear goals;
- are careful and pay attention to details;
- like taking one step at a time;
- have a good memory for facts;
- pay more attention to practical tasks and ideas.

## Strengths

Sensing learners learn best when they can ask their teacher to explain exactly what is expected and when they can focus on skills and tasks that are important in their lives. They like to use computers, watch films or find other ways to see, hear and touch what they are learning.

# Intuitive learners

Intuitive learners:

- like reading and listening;
- like problems that require the use of imagination;
- like variety;
- are more interested in big ideas than in little details;
- like starting on new projects rather than finishing existing ones.

## Strengths

Intuitive learners learn best when they can find ways to be imaginative and creative in school. They prefer to follow their instincts and understand the big picture before they begin school tasks.

# Thinking learners

Thinking learners:

- want to be treated fairly;
- like teachers who are organised;
- want to feel a sense of achievement and skill;
- use clear thinking to work out problems;
- like clear and logical direction.

## Strengths

Thinking learners learn best when they have limited time to do their work and are able to put information in a logical order that makes sense to them. They succeed when they can focus on what they already know in order to make connections to new information.

# Feeling learners

Feeling learners:

- like to have a friendly relationship with teachers;
- learn by helping others;
- need to get along with other people;
- like to work with groups;
- like tasks with which they have a personal connection.

## Strengths

Feeling learners learn best when they can work with a friend, find opportunities to choose topics they care about and help others.

## Judging learners

Judging learners:

- like to have a plan and stick to it;
- work in a steady, orderly way;
- like to finish projects;
- take school seriously;
- like to know exactly what is expected of them.

## Strengths

Judging learners learn best when they have short-term goals, when they are able to make a plan of action and find out from the teacher exactly what is expected.

## Perceiving learners

Perceiving learners:

- are open to new experiences in learning;
- like to make choices;
- are flexible;
- work best when work is fun;
- like to discover new information.

## Strengths

Perceiving learners learn best when they find new ways to do routine tasks in order to generate interest and to discover new information and ideas.

They prefer being involved in projects that are open-ended without definite cut-off points and deadlines.

Studies show that many teachers are of the intuitive type, preferring abstract and theoretical ideas. This learning style preference is often reflected in how they plan for learning in their classrooms. The needs of their pupils, who will have a range of different learning types, are often neglected. We will return to this notion later.

Yet another description of learning style is found in Kolb's Learning Style Model, which classifies individuals over two continuous dimensions as having a preference for:

1. The *concrete experience* mode or the *abstract conceptualisation* mode (the dimension concerning how the learner takes in information).

2. The *active experimentation* mode or the *reflective observation* mode (the dimension concerning how the learner internalises information).

Kolb describes four general learning types based on the two dimensions, as follows:

● *Type 1: Diverger (concrete, reflective)*. Type 1 learners often use the question 'Why?' and they respond well to explanations of how new material relates to their experience and interests. Diverging learners prefer to learn by observation, brainstorming and gathering information. They are imaginative and sensitive.

● *Type 2: Assimilator (abstract, reflective)*. Type 2 learners often use the question 'What?' and respond well to information presented in an organised, logical fashion. They benefit if they are given time for reflection. Assimilating learners prefer to learn by putting information in concise logical order and using reflective observation.

● *Type 3: Converger (abstract, active)*. Type 3 learners often use the question 'How?' and respond to having opportunities to work actively on well-defined tasks. They learn by trial and error in an environment that allows them to fail safely. Converging learners like to learn by solving problems and doing technical tasks, and are good at finding practical uses for ideas.

● *Type 4: Accommodator (concrete, active)*. Type 4 learners often use the question 'What if?' and respond well when they are able to apply new material in problem-solving situations. Accommodating learners are people-oriented, hands-on learners and rely on feelings rather than logic.

Figure 5.2 gives a pictorial explanation of the way that the dimensions interact to give the four learning types.

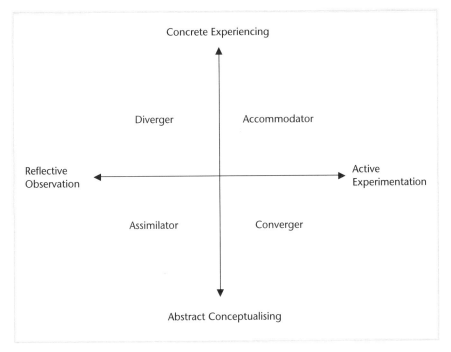

**Figure 5.2** Kolb's dimensions

Kolb says that that, while almost every individual makes use of all learning modes to some extent, each person has a preferred learning style.

The Felder-Silverman Learning Style Model is another system for describing learning style. It has many similarities with the other systems and classifies learners as:

- *sensing learners* who prefer the concrete, are practical, and are oriented toward facts and procedures; or *intuitive learners* who prefer the conceptual, are innovative, and oriented towards theories and meanings;

- *visual learners* who prefer visual representations of material – pictures, diagrams, flow charts; or *verbal learners* who prefer written and spoken explanations;

- *inductive learners* who prefer to consider topics by moving from the specific to the general; or *deductive learners* who prefer to consider topics by moving from the general to the specific;

- *active learners* who learn by trying things out and working with others; or *reflective learners* who learn by thinking things through and working alone;

- *sequential learners* who prefer to work in a linear, orderly fashion and prefer to learn in small incremental steps; or *global learners* who prefer to take a holistic view and learn by taking large steps forward.

## Learning styles and multiple intelligences

Gardner and Hatch conclude that it may be worthwhile for teachers to 'detect the distinctive human strengths and use them as a basis for engagement and learning' (Gardner & Hatch 1990). They describe this process, unsurprisingly, in terms of multiple intelligences, which we have considered in the previous chapter, and in doing so, demonstrate the many overlaps between multiple intelligence theory and the area of study on which this chapter focuses, namely learning styles.

If we look in turn, in Table 5.1, at each of the intelligences and consider the way in which those learners with particular strengths in the area in question might best learn, we can devise a set of ideas which could be of practical use in the planning of learning activities.

There was a great deal of research carried out in the later part of the twentieth century (Dunn *et al.* 1982; Dunn *et al.* 1986; Lemmon 1985; MacMurren 1985) concerned with identifying the relationship between academic achievement and individual learning style. The research has fairly consistent support for the following ideas:

- Pupils do learn in different ways to each other.
- Pupil performance in different subject areas is related to how individuals learn.

**Table 5.1** Learning activity preferences of the different intelligences

| Intelligence | Preferences |
|---|---|
| Linguistic/verbal learner: intelligence related to language and to the written and spoken word | Likes to: read, write and tell stories, work with riddles.<br>Is good at: using descriptive language, memorising places, dates and trivia.<br>Learns best by: saying, hearing and seeing words. |
| Logical/mathematical learner: intelligence related to reasoning, numbers, abstractions and patterns | Likes to: do experiments, work things out, work with numbers, ask questions and explore patterns and relationships.<br>Is good at: maths, reasoning, logic and problem solving, working from concrete to abstract.<br>Learns best by: categorising, classifying and working with abstract patterns and relationships. |
| Spatial/visual learner: intelligence related to anything visual and the creation of mental images | Likes to: draw, build, design and create things, daydream, look at pictures and slides, watch films and play with machines.<br>Is good at: imagining things, sensing changes, mazes and puzzles, and reading maps and charts.<br>Learns best by: visualising, dreaming, using the 'mind's eye' and working with pictures. |
| Bodily/kinaesthetic learner: intelligence related to physical movement and actions located in the brain's motor cortex (where movement is controlled) | Likes to: move around, touch, 'tinker', talk, use body language and perform.<br>Is good at: physical activities and crafts.<br>Learns best by: touching, moving, interacting with space and processing knowledge through bodily sensations. |

**Table 5.1** Learning activity preferences of the different intelligences (cont.)

| Intelligence | Preferences |
|---|---|
| Musical learner: intelligence related to sounds and auditory patterns, to rhythm, beat and tempo | Likes to: play musical instruments, sing, drum. Likes the sound of the human voice. Is good at: listening, inventing tunes, keeping time (tempo), discriminating between different sounds. Learns best by: listening, especially if things are set to music or are rhythmical. |
| Interpersonal learner: intelligence related to relationships with others and various means of communication | Likes to: have lots of friends, talk to people, solve problems and join groups. Is good at: understanding other people's feelings, leading others, organising and communicating. Learns best by: sharing, comparing, relating and talking. |
| Intrapersonal learner: intelligence related to self-reflection and self-awareness | Likes to: work alone and pursue own interests, daydream. Is good at: understanding self, focusing inwards on feelings and dreams, following instincts, pursuing interests/goals and being original. Learns best by: working alone, individualised projects, self-paced instruction and having own space. |
| Naturalistic learner: intelligence related to observation and awareness of the natural world and the patterns to be found there | Likes to: work outdoors, or at least close to the natural environment. Is good at: collecting and classifying, identifying natural artefacts. Learns best by: working outdoors, relating classroom ideas and activities to the natural world. |

- When pupils are taught with approaches and resources that complement their particular learning styles, their achievement is significantly increased.

The third of these points has importance for teachers if they are to develop approaches to teaching all pupils that will ensure that the greatest number of learners in their classes benefit from their teaching. Another interesting but, in the light of what has gone before, possibly quite obvious pointer from research is that children are far more likely to complete their homework if 'its design takes into consideration students' learning styles and study habits' (Dunn *et al.* 1989).

By learning about the learning style preferences of learners, teachers put themselves in a far stronger position when they come to the task of planning learning approaches and classroom activities that are most likely to take advantage of pupils' individual learning styles, which will in turn help them to achieve their learning goals.

Problems can arise for teachers who try to explain things in a way that they consider everyone can understand, when some of their pupils have difficulty in making sense of what they are being taught. From what we have seen, a pupil of a different temperament, whose mind is set in a different way to his or her teacher – in short, with different learning style – is likely to have the greatest difficulty.

It is highly likely to be of great value if both teachers and pupils can have awareness of the potential problems that differences in learning style and preference may lead to. That is, they should (in particular the teacher should) be fully aware that we all learn in different ways, behave in different ways and go about our lives in different ways. We do not have to lose consideration for other people by encouraging differences. Parents too can benefit from knowledge of these differences, as it can impact on the approaches they might take when supporting their children's school work at home.

From the point of view of the teacher then, the important point about learning styles is not to be concerned with how many styles are listed, nor how they might be labelled, but to raise awareness in both teacher and learner that everyone is likely to learn in a different way, and that different learning styles present needs which must be met if teaching is to be effective and learning to take place.

According to Bandler and Grinder (1979), 70 per cent of learners will be able to cope however a lesson is presented; 10 per cent will be unable to learn whatever method is employed, for reasons largely unrelated to learning style; but the remainder will only be able to learn in a visual, auditory or kinaesthetic way. It should perhaps be the view of teachers that 70 per cent is not enough and that some action needs to be taken in order to increase this figure.

## What should we do about this?

One view on the question of what to do with what we have learnt about individual learning styles is summed up by a set of notes found in the psychology department website at Glasgow University:

> Should teachers adapt to learners, or learners to teachers? The answer is 'both'; and the concept to think of is that of learning communities. All (institutional) learning can be thought of from a wholly social perspective, as one of the learner joining a community, and becoming enculturated. From that point of view, the learner needs to do the adapting, and the more they do so, the more they gain access to that subculture and its knowledge.
>
> The complementary viewpoint is that teachers should adapt, not so much to individuals, as to the broadest audience possible; to make their material accessible to the most people.
>
> (Draper 2004)

So, from this perspective, the onus is on both teacher and learner. However, since it is the prime role of a teacher to facilitate and encourage learning in all of their pupils, it is fairly clear that the real responsibility to accommodate lies with the teacher. Naturally though, some accommodating is also required on the part of the learner.

What is perhaps needed is an approach that is sometimes referred to as 'teaching to all types'. This is not always as straightforward as some would have us believe, of course. An example of how to teach to all types, which can also be described as 'appealing to a wide range of learning styles', based on, for example, the Felder-Silverman Model, might look something like this:

- *For the sensing/intuitive continuum:* balance concrete information, such as facts and experimental results, with conceptual information like theories and models and ideas.

- *For the visual/verbal continuum:* make use of graphs, diagrams, pictures and demonstrations as well as spoken and written explanations of the same information; learners can make a choice of which resources to use.

- *For the inductive/deductive continuum:* ask pupils to reason and attempt to explain a general principle given only experimental observations to work with, as well as exploring principles based on their component parts.

- *For the active/reflective continuum:* provide time for pupils to consider the material presented, possibly individually, as well as time for active participation in group work.

- *For the sequential/global learner:* be sure to highlight the logical flow of material but also make connections to other lessons, topics and every-day experiences. Encourage both logical, linear thought patterns and the wider, sometimes referred to as 'lateral', patterns of thought.

There are other, similar sets of instructions which have been prepared for teachers to consider when making plans for learning. The lists refer to learning preferences and suggest particular activities which are likely to satisfy all of, or at least as many of the different preferences that are likely to be encountered. Indeed, Table 5.1 sets out the particular approaches which are likely to be favoured by, and therefore successful with, learners having different preferences and strengths.

We should perhaps bear in mind, however, that the educational system in most countries, and particularly in the developed world, rewards and even requires learning and, in particular, successful learning outcomes in terms of examination passes, to be approached through language – more specifically, written language. This has ramifications for what goes on in classrooms. While teachers have a view to providing appropriate learning activities for a range of different learning styles, they must also have a clear grip on the fact that success in our current educational climate depends heavily upon reading and writing.

## Identifying learning styles

We have seen that it is helpful for teachers to consider the learning styles of their pupils and for them to incorporate what they discover into their approach to planning – at an individual level sometimes. There are formal tests and quizzes designed to identify learning styles and some schools make use of them. There are some examples available online and a simple search will unearth them. Naturally, each learning style 'quiz' or inventory will be designed to categorise learners according to the theoretical position on learning styles taken by its creators. It is possible to find formal ways of identifying learning styles to suit the preferred descriptions of learning styles available, some of which we have considered earlier. There are also similar tests or quizzes available to help in the identification of multiple intelligence strengths and preferences. Some schools or individual teachers like to encourage their pupils to consider their particular learning styles and some of the online quizzes are helpful at this level.

In some cases, teachers do not want to go as far as formally examining the learning styles of a class, but would still like insight into an individual's style in order to be able to better understand how they are likely to function in learning situations. It appears that, at a simple level, it is possible to pick up on some visual cues which give an idea of an individual's style. Put simply, and as we saw earlier, visual learners tend to look up (for a mental picture perhaps), auditory learners tend to look to the side and kinaesthetic learners tend to look down. The reasons for this are not given in any of the easily available sources, but it does seem, as a rule of thumb, to be useful.

There is a possible drawback to helping children to identify their particular learning style: if a child is given a particular learning style label, it is possible that they will centre their learning on this one approach to learning and even refuse to work in other modes. This would be undesirable. When introducing the idea of learning styles to children, it is probably helpful to stress the importance of being able to work and learn in different ways at different times and for different purposes. A case – even a strong case – for encouraging children to develop ways of learning that do not come easily to them can be made.

## Summary

Individual learners have preferred ways of working, thinking and learning. If an individual's preferred approach to learning tasks is ignored in the ways that a teacher expects them to work, there is a distinct possibility that their learning will not progress as efficiently and effectively as it might.

Descriptions of learning styles are plentiful and some are complex. One description commonly used to help teachers understand differences in a practical and immediate way is the 'visual/auditory/kinaesthetic'. It is likely that one-third of any given class will have a preference for learning which is undertaken in one of these divisions. This means that teachers should be aware of and take into account the fact that some of their pupils will find it difficult to make headway with their learning if at least some of it is not presented in an appropriate format for them.

It is very important that opportunities are given to learners of all types to take part fully in the planned learning activities in classrooms and that they should have full access to the curriculum, whatever their learning style preference might be.

 In the classroom

In some ways, the suggestions that might be added at the end of this chapter are very similar to those at the end of the previous chapter, 'Multiple Intelligences'. We have discussed the links between multiple intelligences and learning styles, and it is reasonable to repeat the points from Chapter 4 here:

- Be aware that individuals have different strengths and are likely to perform very differently according to the nature of the style of the tasks with which they are presented.

- Give opportunities for learning in a range of different ways; sitting and listening may suit some children, but others will find this particularly difficult; conversely others will not respond well to individual work. Be flexible in teaching approaches.

● Give opportunities for learners to respond in a range of different ways; writing prose responses is not the only way to record events, indeed there are many ways other than writing that new learning can be dealt with.

● Be prepared to reward responses to work that do not necessarily conform to the traditional expectation of 'school work'.

● Help learners realise that there is more than one way to approach and solve a learning problem, and that one approach is almost certainly as valid as another if it leads to the required outcome.

# Chapter 6

## Brain-based Learning and Other New Understanding

Over the last 20 years or so, there has been an upsurge in both research and interest among educators in what has become known as 'brain-based learning'. As a relatively new area for research and classroom application there is, understandably, some level of disagreement concerning the value of the application of the findings of neuroscience research to classroom practice. However, there is undoubtedly value in some of the claims of the brain learning advocates and for that reason it is of value to spend time here investigating the claims and then some of the suggested approaches to teaching 'with the brain in mind'.

Chipongian (2004) suggests that the term 'brain-based learning' sounds redundant. Even the uninitiated, if questioned, would consider that learning takes place in the brain. She continues to say that: 'Advocates of brain-based teaching insist that there is a difference between "brain-compatible" education, and "brain-antagonistic" teaching practices and methods which can actually prevent learning.' Looked at in the light of this comment, it is perhaps possible to see that there might well be approaches to classroom teaching that might not, for a variety of reasons, be sympathetic to learning – approaches that over-complicate, perhaps, or induce excessive anxiety and stress. As we will see, there are some principles that have developed out of the brain-based learning movement which, if applied, seem to have the potential to improve the learning environment and to lead to improved learning.

First we will look at an aspect of the structure of the brain and the functions assigned by some writers to the left and right hemispheres. Brain research points fairly conclusively to the two hemispheres of the brain having different functions: 'The left brain specialises in academic aspects of learning – language and mathematical processes, logical thoughts, sequences and analysis. The right brain is principally concerned with creative activities utilising rhyme, rhythm, music, visual impressions, colour and pictures' (Rose & Nicholl 1997). Put simply, one hemisphere is predominantly concerned with the logical and the other with the more creative.

It seems that one or other of the hemispheres is dominant in certain activities, but both are involved in almost all of our thinking. This functional difference has implications for how we learn. The problem of brain laterality and the difference in what is known as 'hemispheric dominance' can be seen to relate to an individual's learning style. If an individual has a dominant hemisphere, which seems to be the case in most of us, then the approach taken to mental activity – which of course includes learning – will be affected.

## Left-brain dominance

Those of us who are 'left-brained' tend to favour a slow, step-by-step build-up of information; learning proceeds in a linear fashion.

## Right-brain dominance

Those of us who are 'right-brained' prefer to see the whole picture, to have an overview; learning is a more global or holistic activity.

There are some researchers who set great store by the differentiation of left and right brain hemispheres. Others, while recognising the importance of this supposed difference, and considering it worthy of attention and investigation, are less dogmatic about it.

It is a physiological fact that the brain is made up of two large hemispheres which are joined centrally. The right-side hemisphere controls the motor movement of the left side of the body and the right side of the body is controlled by the left hemisphere. As for the more intellectual functions of the two hemispheres, we are told that it is important not to overemphasise the different functions because the almost infinite complexity of the brain works holistically, with both hemispheres engaged to lesser and greater degrees in all of our mental activity. However, it is important to recognise that 'the two hemispheres operate and process information in very different ways' (Hannaford 1997). Hannaford refers to a 'gestalt' hemisphere and a 'logic' hemisphere. The name 'gestalt' comes from the group of psychologists who described the working of the human mind in a way that suggests that it is capable of working with very large 'whole' events and capable of filling in missing elements of large information sets. The gestalt hemisphere, which in most, but not all, people is the right hemisphere, deals with the whole picture; it operates intuitively and in a more random manner than the logic hemisphere. The logic hemisphere, which is usually the left hemisphere, processes information piece by piece, in sequence and in fine detail.

Each of us has a dominant hemisphere, and this will influence the ways in which we consider the world around us and, naturally, the ways in which we approach learning. According to which hemisphere dominates, we will either prefer to look at the whole picture and operate in an intuitive, more random way, or we will prefer to concentrate on detail and work in a far more ordered and logical way. The background to the left/right-brain account of the ways in which mental activity unfolds actually tells us something which we notice as we interact with people throughout our lives: that is, some people operate in a methodical way, paying great attention to detail, and others are far less well-organised in this respect and operate quite differently. There are also many shades between the two extremes.

There is another aspect of the structure and function of the brain which has a bearing on the theories surrounding brain-based learning. Paul MacLean developed the theory of the 'triune brain', which complements the description of the two hemispheres and their respective functions.

The triune brain ('triune' meaning a trinity or three in one) was first identified in the 1950s, and has been expanded upon in later work (for example, MacLean 1974; 1989). The notion of the triune brain offers a simplified model of the way that the brain functions. It should go without saying that the brain is a highly complex organ, having over 100 billion active nerve cells, each of which is capable of producing 20,000 to 50,000 branches. There are approximately another 900 billion cells which support and protect the nerve cells. The brain functions in a far more complex way than we currently understand and MacLean's model does not purport to do more than illustrate some key elements of the way that the brain operates. The three elements of the structure of the brain, according to MacLean, are:

1. The reptilian or instinctive brain. The reptilian brain controls muscles, balance and autonomic functions (such as breathing and heartbeat) and is always active, even when we are in deep sleep. This part of the brain has the same type of simplistic and instinctive behavioural programs as snakes and lizards, which is where its name comes from. When someone is placed under stress, the reptilian brain takes over. A learner does not respond when the instinctive brain is in control because this part of the brain operates in basic, ritualistic responses, such as flight or fight. We will consider the importance of this aspect of the brain's function in learning situations later.

2. The mid-brain or emotional brain, also known as the 'limbic system'. The role of this part of the brain is to control emotions and it is thought to be the location of the long-term memory. Sometimes referred to as the mammalian brain, this part of the brain corresponds to the brain of most mammals. The mammalian brain is concerned with emotions and instincts, feeding, fighting, fleeing and sexual behaviour. The mid-brain controls such things as the immune system, eating patterns and sleeping cycles. When there is an emotional connection with learning, the mid-brain is engaged and involved. When something connected to a learning experience is funny, sad or exciting, the memory of the event and the likelihood of the learning becoming lasting and meaningful are greatly increased.

3. The neo-cortex is divided into the right and left hemispheres. It is also known as the 'superior' or 'rational' (neo-mammalian) brain. The neo-cortex is close in structure to the brains of the primate mammals. The higher cognitive functions which distinguish humans from the animals are in the neo-cortex. In humans the neo-cortex takes up two-thirds of the total brain mass. The two hemispheres are joined by the corpus callosum which carries messages between the two sides. This part of the brain is involved in problem-solving, discerning relationships and patterns of meaning. The neo-cortex will only function if the other parts of the brain allow it to. For this reason, a calm and composed

environment is essential for learning and in particular for advanced, abstract and creative thought.

There is a great deal more to the brain-based learning movement than the differences between the two hemispheres and the three-part structure. We will now look in turn at some of the main points raised by a new and growing awareness of the role of the brain in learning. We will also consider the views of some of the movement's detractors.

Caine and Caine (1997) have compiled a list of 12 principles for brain-based learning. They explain that these principles are not final and that they should be viewed as evolving. They are drawn from a range of different sources, both original research and writing, and from more recent work based on classroom and other practical research. When reading through the list, it is interesting to think about the source involved. Many of the principles are founded on what has been described in the earlier content of this book. We will consider these as they arise:

1.  The brain is a complex adaptive system.
2.  The brain is a social brain.
3.  The search for meaning is innate.
4.  The search for meaning occurs through patterning.
5.  Emotions are critical to patterning.
6.  Every brain simultaneously perceives and creates parts and wholes.
7.  Learning involves both focused attention and peripheral attention.
8.  Learning always involves conscious and unconscious processes.
9.  We have at least two ways of organising memory.
10. Learning is developmental.
11. Complex learning is enhanced by challenge and inhibited by threat.
12. Every brain is uniquely organised.

(Caine & Caine 1997)

## The brain is a complex adaptive system

The brain can function simultaneously on many levels and in many different ways. The brain is continuously monitoring and processing thoughts, emotions, imagination, predispositions and operating at a physiological level. There is also a neuro-physiological system, which interacts with and exchanges information with its environment and works in parallel with and in conjunction with the other elements that make up the brain. A great many brain functions are hidden from our consciousness – controlling our breathing, for example, and a very large number of other essential activities. As the process of learning is complex and multifaceted, learning can – and should – be approached in a variety of different ways. This idea has certain resonances with what we know about learning styles, and about the importance of the context of learning and the need for learning to be more than mundane.

An example of this idea of variety is that based on the V-A-K description of learning styles by Levine (2003). He recommends transforming a verbal into a visual task and a visual task into a kinaesthetic task. In this way, he suggests that a certain challenge is presented to the brain, not a continuous flow of the same approaches. The notion of 'activity shifting' and teaching to accommodate a range of learning preferences is also considered to be important. Many teachers, in fact, do not need to be told this; changing activity or approach to the same content is an approach advocated by many educators and followed by many teachers. A 'contrasting activity' is often a feature in many lessons. The reason why a contrasting activity is used to good effect can be related to a variety of theoretical underpinnings, not least, the need for challenge and variety.

## The brain is a social brain

The brain responds to social engagement. Work with others can be a stimulus to greater enjoyment of learning and to deeper levels of thought about the topic in question. The notion of the social brain, though not couched in identical terms, can be seen to form a part of the movement towards collaborative learning and working in groups, which has developed out of the work of the social constructivists, including Vygotsky and Bruner, who both stress the importance of dialogue and the use of language as a medium for learning. Learning is deeply influenced by social interactions and relationships.

## The search for meaning is innate

Humans strive to make sense of what they experience, and this can, perhaps, be described as the human brain functioning effectively. Humans instinctively want to know that learning has purpose and value. In part this is a survival instinct. An understanding of the seasons, for example, or the habits of small edible creatures can mean the difference between survival and death. For some this involves a search for meaning in the very nature of creation; for others, at a more immediate level, the need to know why they are asked to complete a particular task in a particular lesson becomes important and this question should be answered. When teachers share with the class the purpose of what they are doing, the learning objectives, not just what they have to do, then the need for understanding and meaning can, in part, be satisfied.

## The search for meaning occurs through patterning

When new ideas are encountered, we make great efforts to link them with prior knowledge and experience which is in some way related to them. This complies with the description of human memory put forward by cognitive constructivist psychologists. Schema theory suggests that new information is linked to and associated with other similar information. If it is difficult to retrieve previously encountered knowledge or experience then learning the new content does not proceed smoothly. Prior knowledge – and in particular the activation of this prior knowledge – is very important in new learning. The links and new associations form ever more complex patterns of knowledge and understanding and it seems that drawing the learner's attention to the structures of their existing schemas and using them to integrate new information facilitates the process of pattern building and leads to more effective learning. The activation of prior knowledge is seen as an essential step preceding the introduction of new material, and opening up a sound foundation for new learning.

The brain seems to have the ability to resist the 'imposition of meaninglessness'. By 'meaninglessness' Caine and Caine (1997) mean isolated pieces of information unrelated to what makes sense to a particular learner.

They continue by saying that effective education must give learners opportunities to generate their own patterns of understanding.

## Emotions are critical to patterning

'Emotional intelligence' was first described by Mayer and Salovey (1990), and further developed by Goleman (1998). Goleman describes emotional intelligence as: 'the capacity for recognizing our own feelings and those of others, for motivating ourselves, and for managing emotions well in ourselves and in our relationships'. Emotional intelligence describes abilities which are distinct from, but work alongside, what can be called 'academic intelligence'.

If an individual is in a state of emotional unrest, for whatever reason, it is likely that he will not be able to function effectively as a learner. Obviously a sensitive teacher will take account of the emotional climate in a classroom, but more importantly, a teacher should ensure that the nature of the classroom and the nature of teaching approaches should not lead to emotional unrest in a class or in an individual. We will consider this further when we review the idea of 'relaxed alertness'.

## Every brain simultaneously perceives and creates parts and wholes

Left/right-brain research is only the beginning of understanding the way the brain divides learning tasks between verbal and visual, analytical and global, logical and creative. Successful teachers engage learners in tasks that require both sides of the brain to engage. An example of this might be using art in maths lessons or music to help the understanding of a scientific principle. In some classrooms, cross-disciplinary approaches are taken, which attempt to embrace the different facets of the brain's structure and function. Sometimes, according to the political climate, this notion of an integrated approach to learning is either promoted or discouraged. Among other things, this can be seen as an attempt to recognise and work with the interaction of both left and right hemispheres.

## Learning involves both focused attention and peripheral attention

The brain takes in information directly, but is also able to give attention to what have been called 'fringe thoughts' (Ruggiero 2000). These fringe thoughts, referred to as 'peripheral signals' by Caine and Caine (1997), can be very potent and can even obscure what should be the main focus of the teaching. We are capable of both paying attention to the main point of reference in a teaching situation and at the same time being aware of many of the peripheral or background events which may be present. This has implications for the classroom environment, since sometimes the peripheral events can take over from the main event, in terms of holding a learner's attention. It also has implications for hidden messages transmitted, sometimes inadvertently, by teachers, via the medium of body language, for example.

## Learning always involves conscious and unconscious processes

At a surface level, it is fairly easy to assess what facts may have been learnt or what new information has been retained. It is far more difficult to assess the depth of understanding that may have developed during the completion of a learning task. There is an enormous amount of unconscious processing taking place in our brains, not just at times of learning, but almost all of the time and more so when there is a conscious effort being made and conscious mental activity is being undertaken. The creation of connections between ideas and growth in conceptual understanding can take time. Often time for reflection is needed to allow for ideas to 'sink in'. This reflection time is a time when ideas can be revisited and reconsidered. Reflection on newly covered work is a time when, sometimes with encouragement, connections can be made and some of the important unconscious processing can be brought to the surface.

## We have at least two ways of organising memory

Differing theories concerning the structure and form of long and short-term memory have been with us for many years. Caine and Caine (1994) refer to O'Keefe and Nadel's (1978) model and explain the two types of memory as taxon/locale and spatial/autobiographical. Taxon/locale memory is motivated by rewards and punishments; recall is not related directly to specific links; and often unrelated information can be accessed in what might appear to be a random fashion. Spatial/autobiographical memory is much more related to the links and associations between events, particularly when personal experience is involved. In this type of learning, recall can be instant and is more reliant on the logic of links formed at the time of the event in question.

These two types of memory help learners to record their experiences, as important and unimportant details are categorised and stored differently. Teachers can attend to both types of memory by organising activities into meaningful parts, placing ideas in context, and incorporating a range of learning styles and multiple intelligences into classroom practice.

## Learning is developmental

Work in the 1980s by Scheibel and Diamond (1986) gave insight into the way that the brain is able to grow and produce more physical connections than it had previously been thought possible. It had been thought that the brain's structure was fixed early in the developmental process and that the growth of new physical pathways was not a real possibility. They describe this ability to grow expansive networks of nervous pathways and connections as 'dendritic fireworks'. This refers to the idea that dendrites – the physical, but microscopic, branches of nerves in the brain which control the movement of electrical nervous impulses – have the ability to grow incredibly rapidly and in many different directions, creating new and complex patterns of neural connections.

## Complex learning is enhanced by challenge and inhibited by threat

For many teachers the notion of differentiation – pitching work at an appropriate level of difficulty for an individual – has become an important element of their work. This has not been done for 'brain-based' reasons. We have come to see, based on the work of Piaget and Vygotsky, that learning will not proceed if the material offered is either too complex or too simple. There is a 'brain-based' explanation, however. If teaching is pitched too low, the brain-based community tells us that the learners will be understimulated. If teaching is at the precise level of the learner, they work in what has been called a 'comfort zone', where little new learning will take place. Teaching at a slightly elevated level, where challenge is provided but the work is not impossible, encourages our learners to engage with the work. This is a very accurate reflection of the work of Vygotsky and the zone of proximal development.

The notion of 'threat' has links to the emotional state of the learner. It is fairly well known that when in a state of stress, induced perhaps by perceived threats of one sort or another, we fail to function effectively. The idea of fight or flight comes into play and it is very unlikely that a child will be able to work at even the simplest level of difficulty in a situation where they are experiencing any sort of negative stress.

## Every brain is uniquely organised

We have seen earlier that individuals differ from one another in a number of ways. This can, in part, be explained by the different experiences that we have, but it is also partly related to the structure and make-up of an individual's brain. Levine (2002) described a 'Myth of Laziness', referring to the perception that a teacher, or other adult, may form of a child based on observed problems with a child's attitude in teaching situations. He suggests that the attitudinal problems, which can result in a number of unhelpful behaviour patterns in the classroom, may stem from a variety of unaddressed problems. Some of the problems may be a result of the unique organisation of the learner's brain. This can be seen to refer to multiple intelligence theory or to notions of cognitive and learning preference. It is possible that some learners, given the right kind of support in organising their learning, through tailored work plans or alternative approaches, can improve their attitudes and behaviour and show marked improvement in their school work. If a small amount of success can be achieved, this can lead to further success and to the well-known benefits associated with succeeding.

Succinctly summarising the 12 principles above, the 'Literacy Organisation', an American non-profit-based group aiming to 'improve American literacy', gives us this short sentence: 'The "brain-based learner" closes down under threat, learns via peripheral events, has a unique brain, learns through both conscious and unconscious processes, has various types of memory, and learns best when content is embedded in experience' (Literacy Organization 2004). Caine and Caine (1997) conclude by saying that: 'Optimizing the use of the human brain means using the brain's infinite capacity to make connections, and understanding what conditions maximize this process.' They identify three 'interactive and mutually supportive' elements that should be present in order for complex learning to take place. The three conditions are:

- an optimal state of mind that we call *relaxed alertness*, consisting of low threat and high challenge;
- the *orchestrated immersion* of the learner in multiple, complex, authentic experience;
- the regular, *active processing* of experience as the basis for making meaning.

(Caine & Caine 1997)

We will look at each of these in turn.

## Relaxed alertness

If it is true that '80 per cent of learning difficulties are related to stress' (Stokes & Whiteside 1984), then it should be seen as an absolute priority for teachers to ensure that the learning environment for which they have responsibility is as stress-free as possible. It is the state of relaxed alertness that, in ideal situations, would ensure a stress-free working environment.

Renate Caine is quoted as saying that: 'If children are to think critically, they must feel safe to take risks' (Poole 1997).

It is generally agreed that teachers should strive to create a 'safe' learning environment for learning to proceed effectively. The requirements for teachers in training in England and Wales (TTA 2003) give a comprehensive and detailed set of standards, all of which must be met, including several that relate to the teaching environment. Standard S3.3.1 states that trainees must demonstrate that: 'They have high expectations of pupils and build successful relationships, centred on teaching and learning. They establish a purposeful learning environment where diversity is valued and where pupils feel secure and confident' (TTA 2003). We all know from our own personal experience that our ability to think coherently can be compromised in situations of even limited stress – job interviews and consultations with medical professionals are two examples of this. This is the case in classrooms when, for whatever reason, children experience negative stress. Some writers emphasise the negative aspects of stress, while others highlight the fact that a little stress is likely to enhance performance. Ellis (1973) describes three varieties of stress: negative stress, distress and positive stress, which he calls eustress. Positive stress, in small doses, can be used in a constructive way; it can lead to heightened performance and alter attitudes and behaviour. It can also have a positive effect on self-esteem. However, the damaging effects of excessive negative stress are to be avoided and the brain-based school of thought considers that stress is, in general terms, counterproductive in terms of effective learning.

## Orchestrated immersion

'Orchestrated immersion' refers to a situation in which children can become fully involved in the topic in question. There are various suggestions about how this might be achieved but, in general terms, topics need to be made interesting and accessible. The idea of orchestrated immersion is clearly related to the notions of context and engagement which were discussed in earlier chapters. It is important that the immersion should be orchestrated, meaning well-structured and developmental, and in the control of the teacher.

## ◼ **Active processing**

Active processing is an important principle and again is related to ideas discussed earlier. As we will see, some of the detractors of brain-based theory comment on the closeness of brain-based precepts to elements of what is known and described in other theoretical frameworks. In the case of active processing, the importance of what the constructivists call 'mental processing' and the emphasis laid on engagement and understanding are clearly very close to each other.

Active processing includes relating what is new to previous experiences and to real-life events. This too is related very closely to the constructivist notion of all new learning being built upon a foundation of what has gone before, and the importance, in practical terms, of relating new to old and 'activating prior knowledge' in order to ease the process of new learning.

Orchestrated immersion and active processing should work together to assist learners in seeing a wider perspective than is sometimes offered in lessons. The ability to connect specific elements of teaching and learning with 'the big picture' is an important part of the brain-based approach.

Situated learning, authentic contexts, the importance of prior learning and engagement – all important in the context of constructivist learning theory – all feature, though in a slightly different guise, in the vocabulary and toolbox of the advocates of the brain-based approach. Also under the broad umbrella of the brain-based perspective, but from a physiological standpoint, there are other important considerations. For the brain to function effectively, there are three important physical prerequisites. These are:

- The brain's need for an adequate supply of oxygen
- The brain's need for an adequate supply of water
- The brain's need for adequate nutrition

The brain also has a need for rest and so the need for sleep in young learners is shown to be very important. All teachers recognise that sleep-deficient children do not make effective learners.

Put simply, the brain needs fuel if it is to function effectively. This fuel comes in the form of oxygen, water and glucose. If any of these are deficient in any measure, then brain function is reduced and eventually impaired. If a child has not eaten any breakfast; if a child sits inactive for lengthy periods, allowing the heart rate to slow to the point where oxygen is supplied in meagre amounts to the brain; and if a child fails to take in adequate amounts of water (we are told that we need to drink between five and eight large glasses of water daily, more on hotter days) then brain performance will drop and the potential for learning will drop commensurately.

The brain is 75 per cent water and even moderate dehydration can cause headaches and dizziness. Promislow (1998) tells us that water:

- heightens energy;
- improves concentration;
- improves mental and physical co-ordination;
- enhances academic skills.

Increasingly schools are becoming aware of the need for water, and are allowing access, in varying degrees of freedom, throughout the school day. Anecdotally at least, many teachers are persuaded of its benefit.

Similarly, with the advent of the Brain Gym movement (Dennison 1986), which, among other things, promotes physical activity through the use of simple exercises based upon primitive reflexes and co-ordination, some schools are finding that the use of movement designed to increase heart-rate seems to lead to improvements in behaviour, concentration and academic achievement. There are reports of gains in attainment and improvement in whole-school behaviour which are attributed to an enhanced programme of PE and exercise in school. Some are included on the Qualifications and Curriculum Authority's website (QCA undated).

Tony Buzan, who is known for his enthusiasm for developing new approaches to learning (see Buzan 1995; 2002), has undertaken extensive work in many different settings concerning the most effective ways to encourage what he considers to be the 'full' use of the brain. He is most well-known for his work on the development of mind mapping techniques, which he describes as the production of a picture or diagram of one's thoughts or conversations. He advocates a pictorial, diagrammatic approach to such activities as note-taking and revision. The approach taken in mind mapping, and perhaps to a lesser extent in concept mapping, is to mimic, at a simplified level, the associative nature of the structure of memory patterns in the brain. The brain, Buzan tells us, operates on a keyword or concept basis and it is extremely helpful, in terms of learning, to emulate this approach.

Accelerated learning is a development in pedagogy which comes in part out of the brain-based learning movement. It relies too on ideas from other areas of research and development in teaching and learning. It is influenced, in particular, by such researchers as Buzan (1995); in the field of memory by Gardner's work on multiple intelligences (Gardner 1993); de Bono's thinking skills (de Bono 1986); Feuerstein's theory of instrumental enrichment (Feuerstein *et al.* 1980); Jensen and the work of many others in brain-based learning; and Sylwester's research on behaviour and stress and the effect of stress on learning (Sylwester 2000).

'Accelerated learning' is an umbrella term for a series of practical approaches to learning which are based on research and developments in aspects of brain function; theories of human attention and motivation; the psychology of learning; and neuroscience. The notion of accelerated learning has the expectation that children can reach a level of achievement which may seem to be beyond their capabilities, if they are effectively prepared and motivated. Based on the precepts of brain-based learning which are described above, accelerated learning expects teachers to:

- Create a positive learning environment. Use visual, musical and physical factors in their organisation for teaching.
- Focus feedback on specific improvements in performance which can be understood and acted upon.
- Give an overview of the content, process and purposes of lessons at the outset.
- Engage learners by setting problems, using real situations and challenging their thinking.
- Provide opportunities for learners to work in a variety of groupings and allow for choice in the way that they record and present their work.
- Allow time for reflection and discussion.
- Spend time reviewing what has been learnt, how the learning developed and how what has been learnt might be used in future.

Smith (1996) uses the acronym NO LIMIT to represent seven principles relating to brain-based learning. The first initial comes from the word k<u>n</u>ow: the learner and teacher should know how the brain works in a learning situation – including that the brain has different parts; that the right and left sides of the brain should be active, connected and working together; that visual, auditory and kinaesthetic inputs can support the efficient working of the brain; and that the brain cannot function without air and water. The second principle refers to <u>o</u>pen and relaxed learners: learning is more enjoyable and longer lasting when the environment is enjoyable and the learner feels confident and comfortable. For example, if music is played during a lesson, this may help to create the right environment for some learners. The third initial is <u>L</u> for learning: by setting step-by-step targets, learners are given a challenging, supportive environment. Obvious and attainable targets can lead to success and experiencing success in achieving targets will motivate learners. <u>I</u>nput, the fourth principle, is based on the idea that a variety of inputs is needed. Smith refers to visual, auditory and kinaesthetic experiences in this context. Next come <u>m</u>ultiple intelligences and the principle that different learners have different intelligences that need to be nurtured and different styles in which they learn. Children may function well in one area – language, for example, where they might even excel – but in other areas they might perform far less well. The sixth principle is to <u>i</u>nvest in several strategies that can improve self-esteem and enhance learning – these are represented by another acronym, BASIS, with five elements: belonging, aspiration, safety, identity and success (Smith 1996). The final initial in NO LIMIT refers to <u>t</u>ry it, <u>t</u>est it and review it – the idea of constantly reviewing work within a system based on and supported by target setting.

All of Smith's principles are said to create a supportive learning environment, with a range of sensory inputs which can motivate learners, enhance their understanding and improve the overall effectiveness of learning.

## Concentration span

The length of time that a learner can concentrate is a crucial aspect of how learning can be structured. In particular, the length of time for which teachers expect their pupils to listen to them can be critical. It is said (though it is very difficult to find research-based evidence for this) that a child's concentration span, in minutes, is equal to the age of the child plus two. It is also said (again without any sort of referenced evidence) that a child's concentration span, in minutes, is the child's age less one. In either case, this is not very long. The average concentration of an American adult is said to be seven minutes, which accounts for the time between adverts in American television programmes, and the British adult concentration span is slightly longer at 11 minutes, although elsewhere it is suggested that the 'average adult' has a concentration span of 20 minutes. All of the easily traceable reports on concentration span seem to neglect to cite their sources.

The fact that children seem to have very short concentration spans is of importance to teachers. Long introductory phases to lessons will fall on deaf ears after the few minutes of concentration have elapsed.

## Detractors

Bruer (1997) gives a comprehensive and rigorously supported argument against the claims made by some of the brain-based learning advocates. He says of some of the ideas which are central to brain-based theory, '... these ideas have been around for a decade, are often based on misconceptions and overgeneralizations of what we know about the brain, and have little to offer to educators' (Bruer 1997). Bruer says that he will examine 'a set of claims that I will call the neuroscience and education argument. The negative conclusion is that the argument fails. The argument fails because its advocates are trying to build a bridge too far' (Bruer 1997).

Bruer is not alone in his concern over the claims made for brain-based learning. Ravitch (2000) calls brain-based learning a troubling trend and a 'distortion of what cognitive scientists have learned about how children learn' (Ravitch 2000). She suggests that brain-based learning might be a commercial bandwagon and that the proliferation of companies offering expensive workshops and resources are evidence of this.

Jensen's worldwide best-seller, *Teaching with the Brain in Mind* (cited in Killion 1999; 2002), in many ways seen as the leading text of the brain-based approach to teaching, has been heavily criticised for its style over content approach, for its lack of scientific rigour and for being an ideas book rather than a research-based factual account.

Despite having some detractors (even such reputable detractors as Bruer), many established educators and researchers give credence to the theory and practice encompassed within the broad scope of the brain-based learning movement. Many teachers who have engaged with only small elements of the breadth of what is included in brain-based learning are reasonably well enough convinced that it makes a positive difference to learning to choose to continue and to develop its use. Many teachers, for example, advocate the implementation of such ideas as the provision of water, intermittent physical activity, an insight into the 'big picture' and the sharing of learning objectives. Many teachers would agree that a relaxed atmosphere is likely to lead to better learning outcomes and strive to achieve such an environment for their classrooms. There are schools where new approaches to much of the delivery of the curriculum are being implemented, based upon some of the brain-based learning principles described here. Time will be the judge of the real efficacy of the approaches, and we must watch carefully to ensure that opportunities for making real headway with teaching and learning are not lost. The neuroscientists themselves are clear that there will be more from their domain in the future. Susan Greenfield, an eminent and well-known researcher of the brain, writing in the *Times Educational Supplement* (TES 2005), says that:

> Brain research is poised, if it can rise to the challenge, to make the biggest contribution of all to how the brain learns through interaction with the environment... Now more than ever before educationalists and brain scientists need to work together.

## Summary

Thanks to detailed brain research, largely undertaken by neuroscientists and related to teaching by psychologists and other interested parties, we have at our disposal a good deal of information about how the brain is likely to function to its full potential. The brain needs food, water and oxygen in order to function physiologically. It appears to need a certain amount of challenge, but closes down under conditions of negative stress. The brain seems to thrive in conditions where activity is encouraged and patterns are allowed to develop. Learning in broad contexts with connections to other areas of understanding seems to be beneficial. Classrooms that provide a safe and stimulating environment, allowing for what are known as 'relaxed alertness', 'active processing' and 'orchestrated immersion', are likely to lead to conditions for effective learning. Obviously these brain-based conditions should exist in conjunction with other conditions for learning which are considered in the other chapters of this book.

## In the classroom

- Allow opportunities to drink water.
- Allow opportunities for movement. Even walking to collect a book from the front of the room is movement. Some determined efforts to encourage increased blood flow are perhaps better than leaving it to chance.
- Do not expect learners to concentrate beyond the limit of their concentration span. Break up activities with short contrasting sections to lessons and have what is known as a 'new beginning'.
- Use activities that challenge different 'brain' strengths – left/right brain.
- Try to give insight into the 'bigger picture' and draw attention to patterns in and between different areas of the curriculum.
- Work towards a learning environment where there is:
  - relaxed alertness
  - orchestrated immersion
  - active processing.

# Chapter 7

## Relating Theory to Practice: What can we learn from research?

Schools exist to promote learning. Teachers are catalysts for learning.
(Cohen, Manion & Morrison 2004)

Since the crucial role of catalyst for learning falls to teachers, it is very important that they have a detailed knowledge and awareness of the ways in which learning can be promoted in schools. This means that teachers need to know about what is currently considered as most important in terms of learning theory and the ways in which the theory can be translated into practice. If we look back at the preceding chapters, we can see that in a teacher's bank of knowledge and understanding about learning there is a place for behaviourism, cognitive and constructivist theory, including situated learning, metacognition, and social constructivism; for an understanding of learning styles and multiple intelligence theory; and for a knowledge of what the neuro-psychologists, and others, are discovering about effective learning contexts. As well as knowing about these areas of theory, teachers must be able to interpret and then apply to practice what it is that they know. In this final chapter we will summarise and review the major components of what has been covered in the earlier chapters and attempt to establish ways of working and organising for learning that will help teachers to provide contexts and activities which will prove to be effective and lead to the promotion of effective – and enjoyable – learning.

Wray and Lewis (1997) single out four aspects of learning which they consider to be of paramount importance. They are:

- Learning is a process of interaction between what is known and what is to be learnt.
- Learning is a social process.

- Learning is situated.
- Learning is a metacognitive process.

We can add that:

- Learning can sometimes proceed in a rote fashion, with less understanding involved initially.
- Learning depends on an individual's preferred learning style.
- Learning depends on certain conditions concerning the brain.

Let us now look at each of the seven points above, and consider more precisely what is meant by each of them and how practice might be affected by them.

## Learning is a process of interaction between what is known and what is to be learnt

What is known (prior knowledge or pre-existing knowledge) is the knowledge, skill or ability that a learner brings to a new learning encounter. This includes all knowledge that is available before the learning event, and which has been gathered or developed by any means, and in any situation, including both formal and, quite often, informal learning situations. Learners need enough previous knowledge and understanding to enable them to learn new things; they also need help making links with new and previous knowledge explicit.

It is considered to be valuable to go through a process of what has been called 'activating prior knowledge'. Teachers often go through this process at the beginning of a new topic. They also use introductory strategies at the beginning of lessons which are continuations from previous lessons. In terms of the practicalities of teaching, this is a process of making children think about the topic or remember what has been covered already. In terms of theory, it is to do with activating particular schemas.

Teachers approach the activation of prior knowledge in a number of different ways. The effective approaches involve what is sometimes referred to as 'elicitation'. This is the process of drawing out from children what they already know, even if they do not realise that they know it.

By careful questioning, a teacher can draw out from individual children, or even large groups of children, ideas, facts and notions which can be of direct relevance to the topic that the teacher wishes to introduce and develop. Other strategies include asking children to bring to mind anything related to a topic. This approach has a number of different names, each having a slightly different shade of meaning: Thought Trawl; Mind Shower; Ideas Meet; and also Brainstorm – now considered inappropriate by some because of its medical associations. Children are asked simply to express ideas, facts or thoughts relating to an idea – 'heat', for example, or 'holidays' – or perhaps to other possibly less abstract notions such as 'pets'; people too can be used to good effect – 'King Henry VIII', for example. Sometimes a list is created; sometimes each offering is discussed. Sometimes the ideas are classified in some way or added to a chart. There are likely to be as many ways of dealing with an activity like this as there are teachers and all are likely to be equally valid. They all serve the same purpose, which is to bring to the forefront of the mind of the individual child, or even to what could be considered a notional group consciousness, what it is that is known about a topic which is about to be introduced and developed through further teaching. For a teacher, the process of activating the prior knowledge of the class is an important exploratory activity. The ideas, facts and thoughts presented by the class can give an important insight, not only into what is known, but also into possible misconceptions which may exist. This is valuable for teachers when deciding precisely which level or, more often, levels of difficulty to plan for, or in helping them to ascertain areas of the topic that seem to be well established and those that are not.

One useful tool available to teachers is known as a K-W-L grid. K-W-L comes from: 'What do I *know*? What do I *want* to find out? What have I *learnt*?' The layout of the grid is largely immaterial. Teachers can provide a framework for children to write in, but this is not always necessary. The activation of prior knowledge element of the grid is the K. Children are asked – and this could be individually, in pairs or in small groups – to write down what they know about a subject. The use of a K-W-L grid will assist the process of activating prior knowledge; with practice children can develop their own, more sophisticated responses to this approach.

The next two elements of the grid are used subsequently, being a means of focusing attention onto specific questions to investigate and then noting the answers to questions formulated in the 'Want to know' section. Table 7.1 is an example of a completed K-W-L grid.

**Table 7.1** Animals in the cold parts of the world

| What do I know already? | What do I want to find out? | What have I learnt? |
|---|---|---|
| 1. Polar bears, penguins and walruses live in the very cold parts of the world. | 1. What other animals live there? | 1. Sea lions and seals. Different sorts of birds. |
| | 2. Do they all fight or do they get on with each other? | 2. Penguins only live at the South Pole and polar bears only live at the North Pole and so they never meet each other. |
| 2. Penguins can't fly. | | |
| 3. Emperor penguins are the biggest penguins. | 3. Can they all swim? | 3. Polar bears are good swimmers. |
| | 4. Are there different sorts of polar bears? | 4. There is only one main type of polar bear. There are lots of different sorts of penguins. |

So the use of such a grid, or a similar approach, can encourage children to focus on what they already know about a topic. It can also allow them to identify what they would like to know about it and then to plan and find something out and note what they have learnt. The K-W-L grid (alternatively known as 'Prior Knowledge and Reaction') was first put forward by Ogle (1989) and has been further extended by Wray and Lewis (1997). It is an example of a device that can be used to good effect when helping children to activate their prior knowledge and understanding.

# Learning is a social process

Provision needs to be made in teaching situations for social interaction and discussion in pairs and other groups of varying sizes, both with and without the teacher taking part. The tradition of learning as a process of discussion can be traced back to Plato and Aristotle but, for a great many years in the more recent history of education, discussion and collaboration have not been encouraged. There are certainly times when children should work quietly and alone, but there are many more occasions when to enter into a dialogue is extremely valuable (Little 1995). The work of Vygotsky and Bruner in particular, and of others, including Bandura, has shown that learning is a process of interaction between learners. The interaction between learner and 'more knowledgeable other' is an important aspect of scaffolding, as is interaction between peers.

Teachers being in dialogue with children, in both whole-class situations and in other groupings, including one-to-one conversations, forms the basis of much good teaching. Different phases of lessons are based to greater and lesser extents on the use of talk, by the teacher but also by the learner. In some lessons, there is a phase of exposition, where a teacher takes on the role of provider of information. This can be a one-way process, but when it involves two-way interaction it is likely to be more effective. The use of focused questioning, particularly the use of different styles of question, should form a part of a teacher's repertoire of approaches to their job. Teachers need to understand and be able to use different types of questions. Using only 'closed' questions, requiring simple one-word answers, will not serve any purpose as far as the elicitation of children's ideas is concerned. Other, more facilitating types of questions should be employed.

Possibly more important than the times when a teacher is in direct dialogue with groups or individuals, are the times when lessons move into a more independent phase; that is, the teacher takes on a less obvious role and children are expected to work under a lower level of supervision from the teacher. During this phase, children can certainly be asked to work individually, but if the opportunity to work collaboratively, in groups of different sizes, is not taken then important learning opportunities are missed. There is a difference between sitting in groups and working individually, and actively working together. Collaborative work implies that there is a shared task which is to be worked on together, either, at a simple level, by discussing the topic and then responding separately, or, at a more sophisticated level, working together to arrive at a collaborative solution or joint end product. For this to be effective, children need support in learning how to discuss and how to collaborate. Tasks need to be succinct, achievable and within the capabilities of the group. Often what we can call the learning styles needs of the individual class members need to be taken into account too. Sensitive teachers will take great care when forming groups and will give opportunities for some children to work alone on occasions. This being said, it is important to give opportunities to learn how to work collaboratively and co-operatively to those who find it difficult. The teacher's role in dealing with this is not straightforward.

There is research to show that the benefits of group work can be great. Mercer (2000), for example, gives a detailed account of the ways in which language can be a medium for effective learning.

In online distance learning situations, dialogue is considered as an essential element of the process of learning. Synchronous (in real time) and asynchronous (exchanges taking place over an extended time period) discussion through the medium of computer conferencing is built into the program of learning in most online courses mediated by information technology. Although this is not directly applicable in most school learning situations, the importance of social contact and dialogue is underlined.

## Learning is situated

Teaching does not take place in a vacuum and all of the parties involved – teachers, children, curriculum and resource developers, and more – bring their own contextual concerns. The context in which learning takes place influences the effectiveness of the learning. A learning context can be analysed in terms of its culture – its values, beliefs and commonly agreed standards. The context can also be analysed in terms of the time of day, the prevailing weather conditions and the immediate physical surroundings. Between these two extremities of definition of context lies a set of important considerations which teachers should take into account. These considerations are to do with the breadth of experience that children bring with them to their learning. Meaningful contexts for learning are very important and it must be remembered that what is meaningful for a teacher is not necessarily meaningful for the child.

Something as simple as using a map of the school or the immediate local environment for an introductory lesson on maps, directions or routes can in some cases lead to far more engagement in the work, and therefore an increase in the likelihood of learning taking place, than if a random or fictitious map is used. When particular work is not progressing as well as had been anticipated, a teacher can always ask a question about the 'setting' of the work, and establish if it might be possible to set the underlying knowledge and concepts in a more generally child-friendly setting. Simple modifications can make big differences.

The customisation of resources is one way of attempting to deal with this concern. For example, putting a set of mathematical problems into the context of a children's television programme which is currently watched by the class can help to stimulate both interest and understanding. The word 'currently' is important here, because a programme that was aired even as few as five years ago might as well be from a hundred years ago as far as primary-aged children are concerned. Another simple approach that can be taken is to use the context of a story that the children are currently reading together or have recently experienced and to make use of text from the story to exemplify particular aspects of language that are being learnt. A page from a favourite book with all of the adjectives missing, for example, can have an interest level and wider appeal to a class of children who have read the book far beyond that of another piece of text.

## Learning is a metacognitive process

A good example of how a consideration of a learning process might be of value to learners is when a class might be asked to learn a list of spellings. (Sadly many spelling lists, which lack the context that might help the process of learning, are presented for learning simply because they are the next set from the 'list'.) For many children, learning spellings is very difficult. If they are not given any guidance in how to learn them, the task can become impossible. There are many different approaches which can be taken, and suggested to children, for learning spellings. Since any given class of children will have a range of different learning preferences represented, it is a sound approach to offer a set of different suggestions. A good starting point might be to ask the class how they go about learning a list. Some children will not have an approach; others will. As we saw earlier, the approaches taken will vary widely, in all probability, from such suggestions as: 'I look at the word and photograph it in my brain, then I know it' to 'I write it out ten times as fast as I can and it sticks in my head' or 'I make up sentences for them and I can remember the sentences then with the words in them.' Simply talking about approaches to this type of learning can make a difference to some children who struggle to learn the words each week. Those who struggle can be asked to devise a way of learning which they will find helpful; it can be based on suggestions from the teacher or on ideas suggested by others in the class. Another way of encouraging thought about learning or mental processing is to ask children to explain how they know something or how they worked it out. In the context of mental arithmetic, for example, listening to explanations of how an answer was arrived at can be an illuminating experience – for both the teacher and the rest of the class alike.

As children get older and the demands made of them increase – in terms of preparation for exams, for example – the approaches that can be taken to revision, and a detailed consideration of what will work best for them individually, become important. An awareness of how best to tackle what can be daunting learning or revising tasks can help to ease the apparent burden. This is true at all levels.

Children's awareness of their own learning, their thought processes, should be promoted. By promoting this awareness, teachers are encouraging metacognitive activity.

## Learning can sometimes proceed in a rote fashion, with little understanding involved

This is perhaps a controversial position to take. What this does not mean is that memorising is the key to learning; this is far from the truth. Understanding should be the aim of education. However, if not 'knowing' certain items of information becomes a hindrance in the process of learning, it can be acceptable to 'drill' the information, in the hope and expectation that, with subsequent well-focused teaching and experience, understanding will follow. Ideally teachers would like young children to know multiplication facts and to understand what it is that they are dealing with. Actually understanding what is meant by 'five threes are 15' is important. Knowing that it could refer to three groups of five or to five groups of three (leading to an understanding of the commutativity of multiplication) and knowing how to work out the answer to the question, 'What is three times five?' should the need arise, is also very important. Having the ability to apply the multiplication fact in a problem with money is something that teachers would also expect. However, if a child struggles to understand, or if understanding progresses slowly and with difficulty, actually being able to respond instantly with the answer '15' in a situation where the result of the multiplication is needed to help towards solving a more advanced problem (concerning area, perhaps) is a very useful ability.

The same can apply in a range of situations in different subject areas. Understanding should be the aim, but recall can be accepted as a valuable halfway house in some cases.

## Learning depends on an individual's preferred learning style

When considering the different preferred styles which individual learners might have, or when taking into account the manifold possibilities when thinking about multiple intelligence profiles, a teacher could be excused for deciding that there are too many variables and too many diverse needs to be met. This is indeed the case, but teachers do need to take into account the needs of the learners in their classes. One of the questions that arise in discussions about learning style and multiple intelligence centres on whether a teacher should match learning tasks to the supposed needs of each learner or whether each learner should be encouraged to widen their learning strategy horizon. Or, in terms of multiple intelligences, the question centres on whether a learner with a particular multiple intelligence strength should be taught with that strength in mind, to the exclusion of approaches which make demands on other intelligences, or should teaching attempt to engage the less strong areas of intelligence in an attempt to strengthen them? The answers to questions of this nature are not easy.

Some would take an extreme position and say that learners with, for example, a kinaesthetic learning propensity should be taught in ways that allow the learner to adopt this style of learning and no other. Some would argue that a learner with high logical intelligence and low linguistic intelligence should have teaching and learning approaches that are aimed at the verbal/linguistic in order that this particular learner might 'improve' in this area. The result of this particular approach could be that this particular learner fails to learn in an effective manner.

There is a modern parable written by George Reavis (Reavis 2000) entitled 'The Animal School'. It relates a time when the animals formed their own school with a curriculum of flying, running and swimming. Those who excelled in any one of the core subjects were given additional teaching in the other subjects, and so the duck was made to spend his time practising running to the point where he became a poor swimmer as a result of the damage caused to his feet. Other animals had similar unfortunate experiences. The animals were obliged to work in the way prescribed and exceptions were not allowed. Any individual strengths or preferences were not taken into account, with the result that most of the animal pupils failed. There are resonances with the parable and the ways in which some formal education is organised, especially in the past but also, we could perhaps say, in classrooms where what is known about learning styles and multiple intelligences is not taken into account.

In a class of 30 or more pupils, it would be very difficult to cater adequately, in every lesson on every day, for each and every individual need. It is sometimes a big enough problem dealing with differentiation in terms of levels of ability in a large and diverse classroom without also providing highly differentiated activities to suit all learning styles and intelligence profiles. So what would a sensible teaching approach look like?

It is generally accepted that teachers should have an understanding of learning style and related areas of interest, and that this knowledge should impact on the ways that teachers plan and teach. Taking into account the difficulties of working with an approach that gives priority to learning style (some of which are considered above), teachers need to provide opportunities for all children to work with their preferred style and within the domain of their intelligence profile of strengths. This will mean allowing for varied approaches at different times and it will also mean allowing for a certain amount of choice on the part of the learners, concerning how they tackle particular tasks and also in how they respond to certain 'requirements' of the teaching.

Some of these choices may appear simple and even trivial, but for some learners they can make a significant difference to the progress of their learning.

## Choice of activity

- Work alone or work with a partner.
- Gather information from books (text or diagrams, tables of statistics), the Internet; an audio recording of a radio programme, a video recording of a television programme.
- Complete a worksheet.
- Solve a problem related to the topic.

## Choice of response

- Individual response or a group response.
- Respond in note form, prose, diagrams or pictures.
- Respond in the form of a creative narrative, even for science in some circumstances.
- Respond in the form of a 3D model.
- Respond in the form of an audio-recorded news item.
- Respond in the form of a video diary.
- Produce and deliver a short presentation (with or without the use of ICT).
- Create a dramatic piece for performance.

All of the above suggested choices relate to one or other learning style preference or multiple intelligence, to greater or lesser degrees. They also are to be found in classrooms in schools throughout the country – there is nothing new in the two lists. However, it is possible that some teachers do not provide a range of different options in their teaching. If, for example, a class is always asked to break into groups of three and discuss the topic in question before responding orally to the rest of the class, a proportion of individual children will be advantaged in terms of their access to the lesson and others disadvantaged. If the response expected to any given work on any given topic is always an individual piece of writing, with a diagram or picture if there is time, the same situation of advantage and disadvantage will exist. Teachers do not need to switch from one approach to another on a roundabout of confusion, but they should be fully aware of the need to cater for the wide range of interests, abilities, propensities and intelligences that will be present in their classrooms. Giving options for ways of working, and for what are sometimes called 'end products', or 'recording', is one way of doing this.

It is very likely that the predominant means of response to a task will remain individual and be in a standard written form. This is a result of the nature of our current educational system, which will change only very slowly, and teachers do need to prepare their pupils for what is expected of them, either in the exam system in later years of education or in adult life. But if learning is to progress in as effective a way as possible, for as many of our young learners as possible, then choice and variety need to be a part of what is offered to them.

## Learning depends on certain conditions concerning the brain

At the very least, it seems that to be receptive to teaching and to be effective learners we need to be well rested, well ventilated and well nourished, including having an adequate supply of water. We can talk either in terms of what the learner needs or what the brain needs, in this case. To supply some of these needs is within the gift of the school. Schools cannot impose bedtimes, nor can they ensure healthy diets (though they can teach about them), but water and oxygen can be supplied very easily: water in the form of access and encouragement, and oxygen in the form of good ventilation and movement of one sort or another.

Teachers can aim to achieve 'relaxed alertness' in their pupils, by the ways in which they organise their teaching and classrooms and the ways in which they respond to their pupils. Teachers can consider what is meant by 'orchestrated immersion' and make decisions about how to best fit this requirement into the experiences that they provide. They can also encourage, by the nature of the tasks they set, the 'active processing' and engagement with facts and ideas which form the core of what it is that they want their pupils to learn.

Based on what we have considered above and in earlier chapters, we can devise a checklist of points which a teacher might consider when planning lessons.

## Lesson checklist

- Is there a clear focus, with explicit learning objectives?
- Is the content based on the pupils' existing knowledge?
- Is the lesson set in an appropriate context?
- Is there scope for social interaction and for activity?
- Is there variety and choice involved in approaches and responses to work?
- Are suitable 'brain-friendly' conditions in place?
- Is the lesson planned in such a way that it aims to move the pupils' learning forward?

Naturally, all lessons will be different. There will be occasions when there is, for example, little opportunity for collaborative work, or limited scope for assuring that the social or cultural context is ideal for the class in question. However, efforts can be made and steps taken to work towards meeting the conditions implied by this list. All lessons need to have a clear focus and aims. Ideally these aims should be made clear to the class. In situations where work continues from one lesson to the next, an opportunity to refresh the aims in the minds of the class should be taken. All lessons should in some way have the purpose of moving on knowledge and understanding; even lessons that are for the purpose of revision can be seen to be moving on and revitalising what has been covered before.

If what has been discovered about effective learning is applied in classrooms, teachers plan and work in a different way from what has become established practice over a large number of years. Teaching approaches will be tailored to what is known about learning and will encompass what has been discovered in recent years about learning and the brain. This will lead to a new learning environment in the classroom when compared with what has gone before. Cohen *et al.* (2004) describe the differences between a more traditional setting and a new, restructured setting as set out in Table 7.2.

'Excellence' and 'enjoyment', the two words in the title of the UK Government's policy for developing the work of primary schools (DfES 2003), sum up what schools can aim for. Children can achieve excellence and in the process derive satisfaction and enjoyment from their work. The excellence may well be a personal excellence and should perhaps be seen as achieving potential, but the enjoyment can be real when they are allowed and encouraged to work in appropriate ways in a school and classroom atmosphere that supports learning and is prepared and maintained by teachers who are aware of the important considerations concerning learning that we have looked at in this book. Learning depends on a certain amount of work on the part of the learner. Teachers, by applying what is known about learning and developing rich learning experiences based on prior knowledge, social interaction, metacognitive ideas, in appropriate contexts and taking into account conditions considered to be 'brain-friendly', are in a privileged position. They are able to take a very strong lead in the process of helping children to reach their potential while enjoying themselves in the process.

**Table 7.2** Extended version of Cohen *et al.* (2004)

|  | **Conventional setting** | **Restructured setting** |
|---|---|---|
| Pupil role | Learn facts and skills by absorbing the content presented by teachers and media resources. | Create knowledge by acting on content provided by teachers, media resources and personal experiences. |
| Curriculum characteristics | Fragmented knowledge and disciplinary separation. Basic literacy established before higher order level enquiry is encouraged. Focus on breadth of knowledge. | Multidisciplinary themes, knowledge integration and application. Emphasis on thinking skills and application. Emphasis on depth of understanding. |
| Social characteristics | Teacher-controlled setting with pupils working independently. Some competition. | Teacher functions as facilitator and learner. Pupils work collaboratively and make some decisions. |
| Assessment | Measurement of fact knowledge and discrete skills. Traditional tests. | Assessment of knowledge application. Performance of tasks to demonstrate understanding. |
| Teacher role | Present information and manage classroom. | Guide pupil enquiry and model active learning. |
| Possible use of the Internet | Source of information for absorption. | Source of information for interpretation and knowledge construction. Outlet for original work. |
| 'Brain-based' and learning style considerations | Very few in evidence; emphasis on listening, reading and writing. | Water available; movement around class encouraged; consideration of pupils' concentration span; variety in approach taken by teacher; choice in response encouraged. |

# Appendix

## Comparing and Contrasting Piaget and Vygotsky – in summary

Both were constructivists.

Both Piaget and Vygotsky believed that individuals actively construct their own knowledge and understanding; Vygotsky stressed the importance of the social interaction in which an individual participates; Piaget stressed the inner motivation to balance new information with existing knowledge and understanding.

# Vygotsky
## Social Constructivism

Children learn through being active.

Learning is a socially mediated activity.

Emphasis placed on the role of the teacher or 'more knowledgeable other' as a 'scaffolder'.

The teacher is a facilitator who provides the challenges that the child needs for achieving more.

Development is fostered by collaboration (in the Zone of Proximal Development), and not strictly age-related.

Development is an internalisation of social experience; children can be taught concepts that are just beyond their level of development with appropriate support. 'What the child can do with an adult today, they can do alone tomorrow.'

# Piaget
## Cognitive Constructivism

Children learn through being active.

Children operate as 'lone scientists'.

If a child is shown how to do something rather than being encouraged to discover it for themselves, understanding may actually be inhibited.

The teacher is the provider of 'artefacts' needed for the child to work with and learn from.

Cognitive growth has a biological, age-related, developmental basis.

Children are unable to extend their cognitive capabilities beyond their stage of development. There is no point in teaching a concept that is beyond their current stage of development.

# References

Bandler, R. and Grinder, J. (1979) *Frogs into Princes*. Moab, UT: Real People Press.

Becker, J. (1993) 'A Model for Improving the Performance of Integrated Learning Systems'. in G. Bailey (ed.) *Computer Based Integrated Learning Systems*. New Jersey: Educational Technology Publications Inc.

Bereiter, C. and Scardamalia, M. (1987) *The Psychology of Written Composition*. Hillsdale, NJ: Lawrence Erlbaum Associates.

Briggs, K. and Myers, I. B. (1975) *The Myers-Briggs Type Indicator*. Palo Alto, CA: Consulting Psychologist Press.

Briggs Myers, I. and Myers, P. (1980) *Gifts Differing*. Palo Alto: Consulting Psychologists Press.

Brown, A. (1987) 'Metacognition, executive control, self-regulation, and other more mysterious mechanisms', in F. E. Weinert & R. H. Kluwe (eds) *Metacognition, motivation, and understanding*. Hillsdale, NJ: Lawrence Erlbaum Associates.

Brown, J. S., Collins, A. and Duguid, P. (1989) 'Situated Cognition and the Culture of Learning', *Educational Researcher*, **18**(1), 32–42.

Bruer, J. T. (1997) 'Education and the brain: A bridge too far', *Educational Researcher*, **26**(8), 4–16.

Bruner, J. (1996) *The Culture of Education*. Cambridge, MA: Harvard University Press.

Buzan, T. (1995) *The Mind Map Book* (2nd edition). London: BBC Books.

Buzan, T. (2002) *How to Mind Map: The Ultimate Thinking Tool That Will Change Your Life*. London: HarperCollins.

Caine, R. and Caine, G. (1994) *Making Connections: Teaching and the Human Brain*. Somerset, NJ: Addison Wesley.

Caine, R. and Caine, G. (1997) *Unleashing the Power of Perceptual Change: The Potential of Brain-Based Teaching.* Virginia: Association for Supervision & Curriculum Development.

Campbell, B. and Campbell, L. (1993) 'Learning through the multiple intelligences'. *Intelligence Connections*, Autumn. Also available at: http://www.multi-intell.com/articles/campbell_article.htm (Accessed 3.1.05).

Carle, E. (2002) [First edition 1969] *The Very Hungry Caterpillar.* London: Puffin Books.

Chandler, D. (1984) *Young Learners and the Microcomputer.* Milton Keynes: Open University Press.

Chastain, K. (1971) *The Development of Modern Language Skills: Theory to Practice.* Chicago, IL: Rand McNally.

Chipongian, L. (2004) *What Is 'Brain-Based Learning'?* The Brain Connection. http://www.brainconnection.com/ (Accessed 17.1.05).

Cohen, L., Manion, I. and Morrison, K. (2004) *A Guide to Teaching Practice* (5th edition). London: Routledge.

Davis, P. M. (1991) *Cognition and Learning: A Review of the Literature with Reference to Ethnolinguistic Minorities.* Dallas, TX: Summer Institute of Linguistics.

de Bono, E. (1986) *De Bono's Thinking Course.* London: BBC Books.

Dennison, P. E. (1986) *Brain Gym.* Glendale, CA: Edu-Kinesthetics Inc.

DES (1982) *Mathematics Counts* (Cockcroft Report). London: HMSO.

DES (1985) *Curriculum Matters 2: The Curriculum from 5–16.* London: HMSO.

Dewar, T. (1996) *Adult Learning Online.* http://www.cybercorp.net/~tammy/lo/oned2.html (Accessed 11.11.04).

DfEE (2000) *Research into Teacher Effectiveness: A Model of Teacher Effectiveness.* Report by Hay McBer to the Department for Education and Employment. London: DfEE.

DfES (2003) *Excellence and Enjoyment: A Strategy for Primary Schools.* London: DfES.

Draper, S. W. (2004) *Learning Styles.* www.psy.gla.ac.uk/~steve/lstyles.html (Accessed 28.12.04).

Dunn, R., Cavanaugh, D., Eberle, B. and Zenhausern, R. (1982) 'Hemispheric preference: The newest element of learning style', *The American Biology Teacher*, 44(5), 291–4.

Dunn, R., Della Valle, J., Dunn, K., Geisert, G., Sinatra, R. and Zenhausern, R. (1986) 'The effects of matching and mismatching students' mobility preferences on recognition and memory tasks', *Journal of Educational Research*, 79(5), 267–72.

Dunn, R., Dunn, K. and Price, G. E. (1989) *The Learning Style Inventory*. Lawrence, KS: Price Systems.

Elliot, S. N. and Busse, R. T. (1991) 'Social skills assessment and intervention with children and adolescents: Guidelines for assessment and training procedures', *School Psychology International*, 12, 63–83.

Ellis, A. (1973) *Humanistic Psychotherapy*. New York: Julin Press.

Feuerstein, R., Rand, Y., Hoffman, M. and Miller, R. (1980) *Instrumental Enrichment: An Intervention Program for Cognitive Modifiability*. Baltimore, MD: University Park Press.

Flavell, J. H. (1976) 'Metacognitive aspects of problem solving', in Resnick, L. B. (ed.) *The Nature of Intelligence*. New Jersey: Lawrence Erlbaum Associates.

Flavell, J. H. (1977) *Cognitive Development*. Englewood Cliffs, NJ: Prentice-Hall.

Fleming, N. D. (2001) *Teaching and Learning Styles: VARK Strategies*. Honolulu: VARK-Learn.

Gardner, H. (1993) *Multiple Intelligences: The Theory in Practice*. New York: Basic Books.

Gardner, H. and Hatch, T. (1990) 'Multiple Intelligences Go to School: Educational Implications of the Theory of Multiple Intelligences', Center for Children and Technology Technical Report, Issue 4. www.edc.org/cct/ccthome/reports/tr4.html (Accessed 12.1.05).

Goleman, D. (1998) *Working with Emotional Intelligence*. London: Bloomsbury.

Hannaford, C. (1997) *The Dominance Factor*. Arlington, TX: Great Ocean.

Hartman, V. F. (1995) 'Teaching and learning style preferences: Transitions through technology', *VCCA Journal*, 9(2), 18–20.

Hoerr, T. (1996) *Multiple Intelligences: Teaching for Success*. St Louis, Mis: The New City School Inc.

Holland, J. H., Holyoak, K. J., Nisbett, R. E. and Thagard, P. R. (1986) *Induction: Processes of Inference, Learning and Discovery.* Cambridge, MA: MIT Press.

Honey, P. and Mumford, A. (1986) *Manual of Learning Styles* (2nd edn). London: P. Honey.

Howe, M. J. A. (1999) *A Teacher's Guide to the Psychology of Learning.* London: Blackwell.

Jensen, E. (1998) *Teaching with the Brain in Mind.* London: Atlantic Books.

Johnson, A. and Kuntz, S. (1997) 'And the Survey Says… How Teachers Use the Theory of Multiple Intelligences', *Classroom Leadership*, **1**(1). Association for Supervision and Curriculum Development.

Johnson-Laird, P. (1983) *Mental Models: Towards a Cognitive Science of Language, Inference, and Consciousness.* Cambridge, MA: Harvard University Press.

Jonassen, D. H., Peck, K. L. and Wilson, B. G. (1999) *Learning with Technology: A Constructivist Perspective.* New Jersey: Merrill.

Killion, K. (1999; 2002) 'Review: "Teaching with the Brain in Mind" by Eric Jensen. At: www.illinoisloop.org/twbim.html (Accessed 21.1.05).

Lave, J. and Wenger, E. (1991) *Situated Learning.* Cambridge: Cambridge University Press.

Lawrence, G. (1994) *People Types and Tiger Stripes* (3rd edn). Gainesville, FL: Gainsville Center for Applications of Psychological Type.

Leadership Project (1995) *Adult Learning Principles & Practice.* Toronto: Sheridan College.

Lemmon, P. (1985) 'A school where learning styles make a difference', *Principal*, **64**, 26–9.

Levine, M. (2002). *The myth of laziness.* New York: Simon and Schuster.

Levine, M. (2003) *A mind at a time.* New York: Simon and Schuster.

Literacy Organisation (2004) Talking Page. www.talkingpage.org/ (Accessed 8.1.05).

Little, D. (1995) 'Learning as Dialogue: The Dependence of Learner Autonomy on Teacher Autonomy', *System*, **23**(2), 175–81.

McFarlane, A. E. (1997) 'Thinking about writing', in McFarlane, A. E. (ed.) *Information Technology and Authentic Learning.* London: Routledge.

MacLean, P. (1974) *Triune Conception of the Brain and Behaviour*. Toronto: University of Toronto Press.

MacLean, P. (1989) *The Triune Brain in Evolution: Role in Palaeocerebral Functions*. Dordrecht: Kluwer Academic.

MacMurren, H. (1985) 'A comparative study of the effects of matching and mismatching sixth-grade students with their learning style preferences for the physical element of intake and their subsequent reading speed and accuracy scores and attitudes'. Doctoral dissertation, St. John's University, New York.

Mayer, J. and Salovey, P. (1990) 'Emotional Intelligence', *Imagination, Cognition and Personality*, **9**, 185–211.

Mayer, R. E. (1983) *Thinking: Problem Solving and Cognition*. New York: W. H. Freeman & Co.

Mercer, N. (2000) *Words and Minds: How We Use Language to Think Together*. London: Routledge.

New City School (2004) http://www.newcityschool.org/innovations/mi/linguistic.html (Accessed 17.1.05).

Ogle, D. M. (1989) 'The "Know, Want to Know, Learn" Strategy', in Muth, K. D. (ed.) *Children's Comprehension of Text*. Newark: International Reading Association.

O'Keefe, J. and Nadel, L. (1978) *The hippocampus as a cognitive map*. New York: Oxford University Press.

Poole, C. (1997) 'Maximising Learning: A Conversation with Renate Nummela Caine', *Educational Leadership*, 54(6).

Posner, M. (ed.) (1984) *Foundations of Cognitive Science*. Cambridge, MA: MIT Press.

Promislow, S. (1998) *Making the Brain/Body Connection*. Ontario: General Distributing.

Purcell, I. (undated) *Integrated Learning Systems – Do They Enhance Learning?* Found at: www.cbltwork.soton.ac.uk/purcell/prin/#section2 (Accessed 1.12.04).

QCA (undated) www.qca.org.uk/pess/8.htm (Accessed 1.2.05).

Ravitch, D. (2000) 'Hard Lessons: An Interview', *Atlantic [Monthly] Online*.

Reavis, G. (2000) 'The animal school', in Caufield, J. and Hansen, M. V. (eds) *Chicken Soup for the Soul: Stories that Restore Your Faith in Human Nature*. London: Vermillion.

Reid, J., Forrestal, P. and Cook, J. (1989) *Small Group Learning in the Classroom.* Scarborough (Australia): Chalkface Press; London: English and Media Centre.

Rose, C. and Nicholl, M. J. (1997) *Accelerated Learning for the 21st Century.* New York: Dell Publishing.

Ruggiero, V. R. (2000) *The art of thinking: a guide to critical and creative thought.* Somerset, NJ: Pearson Longman.

Scheibel, A. and Diamond, M. (1986) *The Human Brain Coloring Book.* New York: HarperCollins.

Selinger, M. (2001) 'Setting Authentic Tasks Using the Internet', in M. Leask (ed.) *Issues in Teaching Using ICT.* London: RoutledgeFalmer.

Sewell, D. (1990) *New Tools for New Minds.* London: Harvester Wheatsheaf.

Skinner, B. F. (1958) 'Reinforcement Today', *American Psychologist*, **13**, 94–9.

Smith, A. (1996) *Accelerated Learning in the Classroom.* Stafford: Network Educational Press Ltd.

Stokes, G. and Whiteside, D. (1984) *One Brain: Dyslexic Learning Correction and Brain Integration.* Burbank, CA: Three In One Concepts.

Sylwester, R. (2000) *A Biological Brain in a Cultural Classroom.* Thousand Oaks, CA: Corwin Press, Inc.

Teaching and Learning for Life (2000) Website at: http://www.gigglepotz.com/miplans.htm (Accessed 30.1.05).

TES (2005) 'Answer rich, question poor: Susan Greenfield – Teaching and Learning Supplement', *Times Educational Supplement* (28.1.05).

TIP (undated) The Theories in Practice Website at: http://tip.psychology.org/gardner.html (Accessed 17.1.05).

TTA (Teacher Training Agency) (2003) *Qualifying to Teach: Professional Standards for Qualified Teacher Status and Requirements for Initial Teacher Training.* London: TTA.

Underwood, J. and Brown, J. (eds) (1997) *Integrated Learning Systems: Potential into Practice.* Oxford: Heinemann.

Underwood, J., Cavendish, S., Dowling, S., Fogelman, K. and Lawson, T. (1994) *Integrated Learning Systems in UK Schools: Final Report.* Leicester: Leicester University, School of Education.

Woolfolk, A. E. (1993) *Educational Psychology.* Needham Heights: Allyn and Bacon.

Wray, D. and Lewis, M. (1997) *Extending Literacy.* London: RoutledgeFalmer.

# Index

An 'f.' after a page number indicates a figure, or figure and text; a 't.' indicates a table, or table and text.